KU-164-671

The PRISONERS of
VORONESH

*The Diary of Sergeant George Newman,
23rd Regiment of Foot
The Royal Welch Fusiliers
taken prisoner at Inkerman*

Transcribed and Edited by
DAVID INGLESANT

UNWIN BROTHERS LIMITED
and
The Trustees of the Regimental Museum,
THE ROYAL WELCH FUSILIERS

The Gresham Press
OLD WOKING, SURREY, ENGLAND

THE PRISONERS OF VORONESH, transcribed and
edited by David Inglesant

ISBN 0 905418 14 X

© David Inglesant, 1977

Printed by
UNWIN BROTHERS LIMITED
The Gresham Press, Old Woking, Surrey, GU22 9LH,
England

THE PRISONERS OF VORONESH

CONTENTS

ILLUSTRATIONS

PREFACE

MAJOR GENERAL P. R. LEUCHARS, C.B.E.
Colonel, The Royal Welch Fusiliers

How fortunate it is that there are some of us who do not destroy, but treasure and preserve things which, at first sight, appear of little significance.

Such are the old school exercise books in which Sergeant Newman wrote the account of his adventures when taken prisoner of war by the Russians at the Battle of Inkerman in 1854. We are fortunate indeed, not only that they have survived, but also that Mr. Inglesant has been able, by such painstaking work, to present us with a most readable story of the adventures of a sergeant whose natural instinct to survive most dreadful hardships was fortified by a tremendous pride in his regiment.

The experiences of others who were prisoners in Russia were recorded many years ago and the events they described emphasise the veracity of Sergeant Newman. His account is not embroidered and must be an inspiration to all those who admire a true tale of adventure.

Caernarvon, 1977

INTRODUCTION

The original manuscript was beautifully written in Newman's own hand, in two exercise books, subsequently bound into one volume. There was no break in the narrative and I have therefore had to divide it into chapters and paragraphs to make it more acceptable to the general reader.

Newman's style is so descriptive, his memory so clear and his concern for the people and places he tells about so perceptive that I have tried not to break the flow of the original. Only where I felt it necessary to explain particular statements have I done so. Such notes I have included in the text so that it can be read without the interruption of footnotes.

I have retained some of Newman's spelling, to keep the flavour of the original.

I am particularly indebted to Diana Marcham for allowing me free use of the original manuscript. Also, to Vera Marstrand, John Innes and the Librarian and staff at London University School of Slavonic and East European Studies, for help with research into Russia. To the Librarian and staff of the Staff College, Camberley, and the National Army Museum for help in the military aspects. And, to Major Kirby, curator of the Royal Welch Fusiliers' Museum, and Hagan Powell of Unwin Brothers for their helpful suggestions and unfailing courtesy and patience.

DAVID INGLESANT

Puttenham, Surrey, 1977

THE 23RD ROYAL WELCH FUSILIERS
AT THE BATTLE OF THE ALMA

PROLOGUE

George Newman was born in April 1828, at Runcorn in Cheshire. His early life is a complete mystery. He certainly went to France, where he learned the language.

On the 8th of February 1849, at the age of 21 he enlisted in the 23rd Regiment of Foot, The Royal Welch Fusiliers, then at Winchester. In the Muster Rolls he is described as being $5'8\frac{1}{2}''$ tall. He was given the Regimental number 3252, and a bounty pay of £4.

On the 14th of January 1854 he was present at the wedding of his half-brother, William Peerless, for whom he was later to write his diary. In March of that year war was declared on Russia and on the 5th of April he sailed with the Regiment for the East.

At the Battle of Inkerman, on the 5th of November, he was taken prisoner, and remained in Russian hands until October the following year.

After the war he returned to England and is mentioned a number of times in the Regimental Muster Books and Pay Lists. On the 1st of January 1857 he went on furlough.

There is no further information about him. Like millions, he passed unrecorded into history, save for his diary.

He wrote this shortly after the war for his half-brother, who died during the writing of it. It passed to their sister, Hannah Peerless, who had married, in 1856, Isaac Hinton. Their youngest son was father of Dorothy Riley, whose daughter, Diana, has it now.

Information about George Newman is scant indeed.

Information about the Crimean War is plentiful. The causes were complex, but the spark which started it was a minor squabble about the custody of the holy places of Jerusalem and Bethany. At that time they were part of the Turkish Empire. The problem could not be settled amicably and, in July 1853, the Russians, champions of the Orthodox Church, marched on Turkey's northern border. A month later the Turkish Black Sea Fleet was sunk, in harbour.

Britain and France, furious at such blatant aggression by so powerful a nation, declared war on Russia in March 1854. After a short campaign on the western seaboard of the Black Sea, the allied armies embarked for the Crimean Peninsular. Here was the principle threat, the powerful garrison and harbour of Sebastopol.

Sergeant Newman's regiment, the Royal Welch Fusiliers, had carried their colours with distinction through almost every great campaign since 1689, and had won many battle honours. They were about to add three more in the Crimea.

He was with them when they landed in the Crimea, as part of the famous Light Division. Confronted by the Russians barring the road to Sebastopol, the Division was at the forefront of the successful but costly Battle of the Alma. The casualties suffered by the 23rd were frightful and George Newman was fortunate not to be among them.

He was with them when they marched on Sebastopol itself and took his share in the opening weeks of that terrible siege.

On the 5th of November 1854 the Russians made a great counter-attack on the British position but were repulsed and the battle became known as the Battle of Inkerman. Much of it was fought in swirling mist and consisted of isolated engagements, often hand-to-hand and on local initiative. It is also called the 'Soldiers' Battle'.

An outpost of the Royal Welch Fusiliers, under the command of Lt. James Duff was in a small valley known as the White House Ravine. He had with him twelve privates. Sergeant Newman was a member of this party. It was an isolated position and contemporary records of the Royal

Welch state that the heights on the right had been left unguarded.

Emerging from the heavy morning mist the Russians were therefore able to surround Lt. Duff and his men and it was not long before they were completely overwhelmed and made prisoners of war.

It is at this moment that the diary begins.

CHAPTER ONE

*Inkerman
5th November 1854*

four feet upwards and then fall,
, others fell foward at once with
r moved more, others who were hi
art would drop their firelocks an
part with their hands and mak
d moans, many of this class were b
ounded limbs up the ravine in th
going, I never expected to have g
ive, but by Gods mercy I did, although
rough my great coat which I had
alf way up the small ravine when
mp of a russian with a tremendo
t me with his firelock clubbed i
fellow on my right with the en
before me in an attitude of fight
w him to touch me, there was o
them but the man on my left i
led me past while my cutlass frie
e, this was the only time that v
me and we reached the top of th
the shot while flew quite fast en
now got into the range of the ar
ot and shell whistled and ex
urrily I assure you, As we went on
eral dead bodies of Russians w

I found myself marching to the rear of the Russian army, most kindly escorted by a bodyguard of three men, one having a tight hold on my right wrist, another my left, and one following behind me with his bayonet at the 'charge', of which he would now and then give me a gentle prick about my great seat of honour, just to remind me, I suppose, that he was on the alert. The man on my right carried my rifle and bayonet and the one on my left had a drawn cutlass in his hand.

The road took us up a small ravine, leading from the Careening ravine to the top of the plains of Inkerman, and the whole road was swept by our riflemen, of whom three companies were extended on the heights near the redoubt and in rear of the Five Gun battery. They were pretty well concealed by the brushwood and commanded the whole of the small ravine up which we were taken. The Russians were very thick in this place and afforded an excellent bit of shooting for our riflemen. Some, when they were struck, would bound three or four feet in the air and then fall heavily to the ground; others fell forwards at once with their arms outstretched and never moved more. Others who were hit in not a vital part would drop their firelocks and clasp the injured part with their hands and make dreadful cries and moans. Many of this class were trying to drag their wounded limbs up the ravine in the direction we were going. I never expected to get out of the place alive, but by God's mercy I did, although I had five balls through my greatcoat, which I had on me.

The British Army had recently been equipped with the French Minie rifle, superior in every way to the smooth-bore musket and capable of the accuracy described.

I was about half-way up the ravine when a thumping great lump of a Russian, with a tremendous howl, made a run at me wielding his firelock like a club, but the fellow on my right with the cutlass threw himself before me in an attitude of fight and would not allow him to touch me. There was a great row between them, but the man on my left and Mr. Bayonet behind led me past, while my cutlass friend confronted my big foe. This was the only time that violence was offered me and we reached the top of the plain in safety.

The shot flew fast enough, and we now came into range of the Artillery and their shot and shell whistled and exploded about us very merrily, I assure you. As we went on we came upon several dead bodies of Russians who had been killed on the 26th October, when they attempted to make a reconnaissance of our quarters. My companions pointed them out to me with a grin—and I saw they were putrid, of which my nose soon gave me notice, as they stank awfully, and were quite black and some of them naked.

He is here referring to 'Little Inkerman', on the 26th October when, at half past one in the afternoon, 5,000 Russians, with four light guns left Sebastopol and occupied Shell Hill, a prominence in the middle of the Inkerman ridge. A picket of the 49th and 95th, heavily outnumbered, had fallen back on the light defence known as 'the barrier' and the British Gunners had soon opened up. Within three hours the Russian guns had been destroyed and they were forced to retire, with a loss of 250 killed and 80 prisoners. Nonetheless they had gained valuable information about the British defences.

We were getting pretty well to the rear and I observed a group of mounted officers in front of me on a small hill. They were a General and his staff. As we got nearer the General came towards us and, coming up to me, asked me in good

English if I was a Frenchman. I answered that I was English. Then he said,

"Haven't we hit the Duke of Cambridge's Division nicely?"

I answered that he had so, and he then said,

"Did you expect this attack?"

I answered in the negative and then asked him what they intended to do with us.

"Oh, you'll be taken care of," said he.

"I suppose so," said I, "for a day or two, to see what you can learn from me and then shoot me."

"Oh, no," says he, "you'll be kindly treated, and now, good day."

With that he lifted his cap to me and rode off towards the front. A condescension that rose me a great deal in the estimation of my guard, who, I believe, thought me an officer after.

The Duke of Cambridge, the Queen's cousin, was, at 35, the youngest of the Crimean Divisional Generals and commanded the First Division, including the Brigade of Guards. At this point of the battle only a roving picket of the guards had been involved, the Light and Second Divisions bearing the brunt of the attack. Certainly Sgt. Newman would not have been able to tell one way or another. The Russian General probably thought that the First Division had already been engaged.

A short distance further on I met another General who asked me in French if I was a Frenchman. I told him that I was English, but he asked me how many men we had and I told him seventy five thousand. At the same time I do not believe that the whole of the English army would have mustered fifteen thousand efficient men. He then said something in Russian to my escort and rode off, and I was led some distance further.

In fact, the total British troops before Sebastopol was 22,000.

We descended a hill, when we came upon a circle of men of several regiments, seated on the ground—with Capt. Duff in the centre—smoking their pipes and paper cigarettes given them by some of the Russian officers. I was joyously welcomed by all and Mr. Duff gave me a cigar and told me to sit down by him, which I did and had a good smoke—the Russian officers and men standing round in a circle.

The smoking of paper cigarettes was an exclusively Russian practice at the time and would have been unfamiliar to Newman and his comrades. However, the taste for these cigarettes formed by soldiers in the Crimea led to their introduction into England for the first time and consequently the foundation of a considerable industry.

Capt. Duff told me that they had greatly ill-treated him after he was taken, and several of the party besides, and one of them had stolen his ring, a valuable family relic.

"And there he stands now, with it on his finger," said he, pointing to the man. A Russian officer soon came up and finding that Duff could speak French well entered into conversation with him. Capt. Duff told him about the ring and pointed out the man to him; then the officer went over to the fellow and took the ring from him and gave him a tremendous quitting, and gave the ring back to our Captain.

We stopped in the place about two hours, and during the whole of that time vast masses of the enemy infantry and tremendous trains of artillery poured past us in the direction of the fight, and the din of battle became louder and louder, while hundreds of wounded were brought by or staggered past us. I noted that the whole of their officers had got the rough greatcoat on, the same as the soldiers, and some had even got cross belts and carried a firelock and bayonet, like the men. The only outward sign of their being officers was the hilt of their swords on the outside of their rough coats. I felt certain at the time, and have since found out beyond doubt, that they disguised themselves thus to avoid being a conspicuous mark for our men.

After two hours' rest we were marched on again, and led along the bank of the harbour to the bridge that crosses the Chernaya river at the top end of the bay. When we reached it we were obliged to halt, for the bridge and long plank road on the other side was completely choked with artillery and ammunition wagons all pressing onwards to the fight.

Sebastopol was one of the greatest fortified dockyards in the world. Like Balaclava the town and harbour lay around the southern shores of an inlet. On the northern shore, in defence of the harbour, extensive fortifications, including the great Fort Constantine and five other batteries, had been completed, forming now a major supply and maintenance area for the Russian army. In 1832 the Russian Government had engaged the services of an English engineer, Col. Upton, to build three huge dry docks for the harbour. As part of the work it was decided to build an aqueduct to bring fresh water from the river Chernaya to these docks, because the water in the harbour had been found to contain a virulent little worm which attacked the timbers in the ships' bottoms and made them unservicable in two or three years. The work cost £15,000 and there were three aqueducts and 800 ft of tunnelling. Unfortunately, when completed, it was discovered that the worm actually came from the river itself. The bridge which Newman describes passed over this canal as well as the river, and the road led onwards to the plank road, which the Russians had built over the marshes.

The ammunition and artillery wagons referred to were part of the army of 13,500 men and 96 guns under General Pauloff on the Russian left, coming up to assist the already engaged Soimonoff attack.

While we remained here I observed what had been done with their wounded. A large, flat-bottomed barge was in the river, made fast to the bridge, into which the wounded were put by scores, and, when full, taken down into the bay a short distance and the wounded put on board a steamer which took them to Sebastopol. There were two steamers at this work and I saw several barge loads taken away while I remained there.

We were here joined by several Frenchmen, who were taken that morning in an attempt at their works, among them two Zouaves, wounded, and a little French sergeant, who spoke a little English, for he had been employed in some English establishment in Paris before joining the army. I shall have to speak again of this sergeant, so I shall tell you his name—it was Le Marche, I forget his Christian name.

Situated to the left of the British lines the French were not directly involved at Inkerman. However, since the lines joined near the Victoria ridge it was inevitable that a few would be engaged and their timely intervention was most welcome.

We remained here about an hour, during which time Capt. Duff was surrounded by the officers of a regiment who had halted close by apparently waiting for an order to move forward. I understood a great deal of what was said and found out that we should be sent up the country. Mr. Duff introduced me as his sergeant, and I was soon presented with some cigars and a good pull of what they were pleased to call 'eau-de-vie' from a large flask. At length the regiment got orders to move, and we also, only we went a different way, for they climbed the hill to go the fight, while we were moved over the bridge away from it.

When we got over the bridge and plank road, we found ourselves at the foot of a steep hill and small plain among a few more regiments (which I believe were here kept in reserve) and a large number of Cossacks and a great many wagons loaded with gabions and driven by peasants, who looked anything but comfortable at being so near to such a piece of work.

The Crimean Peninsular had only been conquered by Russia in 1783, and the Crimean Tartar peasant had a hearty dislike and fear of his Russian masters.

Gabions are cylindrical wicker baskets, open at both ends and varying in size, used for lining interiors of batteries.

In front of us was the field of fight, but we could not see it then as it was on the hills and we were in the deep and wide valley of the Chernaya, but the shells from our artillery were continually exploding in the air above us, and, as the day drew to a close we saw the last of the battle quite plain; but more of this presently.

When we reached this place we again sat down in a circle with the same amusement as before, smoking cigarettes and staring at the circle of Russians—and they at us. Some of the men managed to save their haversacks and we soon polished off what biscuits were in them. The Russians now began to bring us a lot of our wounded who had been taken that we might minister to their wants. We had fourteen of them in all and most belonged to different regiments. Capt. Duff tried to get a doctor to them but without effect.

It was now getting late in the day and the tide of battle was rolling nearer to us. We could see the smoke and we watched for the issue anxiously. In the meantime, large bodies of the enemy were descending from the fight, not running but out of all order and making for the bridge with the plank road, until this was crowded to excess by the troops and artillery and the barge could not take the wounded fast enough and they came staggering among the crowd, shrieking and groaning terribly; but no one took the least notice of them. As the men got over the plank road they formed into a large crowd—no order or discipline, but still getting thicker and denser every moment so they could not move.

The battle drew nearer and nearer and now we could see the flames from the firelocks and the grey-coated enemy retiring down the side of the hill towards us—and now another line appears on the hills over them and a tremendous flash and roar of musketry, and then we could see them—ours—following them down the hill, while the flashes from their pieces were incessant. My very blood boiled in my veins through the excitement, and I cursed hard fate that held me from being among them. I looked round carefully for a chance to escape, but the bridge was blocked up with thousands of men descending the hills on the far side, and we were surrounded where we stood, so I had no chance . . . but to return to the field of fight.

I watched the whole of the finish very anxiously, and presently saw several bodies of men on the crest of the hill. I knew what they were directly and pointed them out to Capt. Duff with the words, "We shall have it directly, sir."

The words were scarce out of my mouth when we could see the flash of the gun and the next instant a shell pitched right in among the crowd close to us. Another and another and many more followed in rapid succession, and I and the rest, even the wounded, could not help saying, "Go to it, you devils—give it to 'em"–not thinking that they were just as likely to give it to us as to the Russians.

And now the tumult that ensued—the wagons of gabions upset, some by the shot and shell and some by the soldiers, to make room for the wounded; the soldiers scattering all over the hills and along the valleys as quick as their legs could carry them; the cries of the wounded for help; the peasants' horses taking fright at the explosions of the shells, and kicking right and left, while every instant kept adding to the number of the killed that day.

He was here facing the steep escarpment, rising above the river Chernaya, pierced by several gulleys, about the heads of which some of the fiercest fighting took place. Facing the British had been Pauloff's main force—now reduced to about 6,000 men, and against them was ranged the British 2nd Division and the Brigade of Guards: Grenadiers, Scots Fusiliers and Coldstreams. By about 11.00 a.m., however, the Russians had been forced to the edge of the plains, but the British were very hard pressed. At General Raglan's request General Bosquet sent in his Zouave and Algerian regiments. Charging forward together, the Guards and French drove the Russians from the plains.

"Mon Dieu, quel abattoir" ("My God, what a slaughter-house"), exclaimed General Bosquet, but this infusion of French troops was sufficient to secure success and everywhere the Russians went streaming back to their own lines, whilst the allies remained in command of the heights.

The time was about 2.00 p.m. and the battle of Inkerman was won.

CHAPTER TWO

Into Captivity
5th – 8th November

THE BATTLE OF INKERMAN. *5th November 1854*

An officer of Cossack rode up to us and shouted and made signs to us to take up our wounded and toddle, which we did in the best manner possible. Some we managed to get to the wagons, and then those who had blankets spread them on the ground and placed the wounded on them, with three to carry one, two being at the head and one at the foot; and we moved off as quickly as possible, Capt. Duff and myself stopping to see the others off.

We then had several wounded left and did not know what to do with them, but the Captain noticed one of the men, who was helping to carry another with a blanket strapped to his back, and told me to make my way to him and get the blanket, as he would help me carry one more. I got the blanket and Capt. Duff picked out a sergeant of the 1st Battalion of the Rifles, who was shot through the body. The ball, to all appearances, must have gone close to the heart and I did not expect he would have lived another hour, but he did and got well and came back from Russia with us. His name was George Noseley. We carried him along on the blanket between us through the crowd and shells and shot for some distance— perhaps half a mile—when some of our men, having got rid of the burdens, stopped until we came up and gave us their assistance, and we soon got out of range of the guns.

The Rifle Brigade fielded two battalions at Inkerman. The 2nd Battalion was with the Light Division and the 1st Battalion with the 4th Division. Fighting alongside the 57th Regiment, the 1st Battalion was instrumental in recapturing Shell Hill, which the Russians had taken earlier in the morning.

Colour Sergeant Noseley, dangerously wounded, was taken prisoner. He had served in the Kaffir wars of 1852–3, was to survive the Crimean War and be commissioned in 1858. He was promoted Lieutenant in 1863, Paymaster in 1864, and retired on half-pay as Major in 1877.

A few minutes after we came up with our party, who were halted by the side of the road, and a Russian Officer standing with them. He spoke to Mr. Duff and saw some wagons coming loaded with wounded Russians. He halted them, had the Russians taken out and our men put in, a proceeding that gave anything but pleasure to the wounded Russians, for those who could drag their limbs along anyhow were obliged to do so, and those who could not were obliged to stop where they were.

I shall never forget the sight one poor wounded fellow presented. My attention was drawn to him by the horrible noise he was making, and looking at him I saw his mouth was wide open as though he could not shut it. The blood was running in two streams from either side of his mouth. A shot, and it might have been a small grape or large cannister by the size of hole it made, had entered his mouth and gone through the lower part of the back of his head, taking away his teeth and tearing his tongue from the bottom jaw and forcing it through the wound behind, where it protruded in what I thought awful mockery of the poor fellow's suffering. I did not study such a picture long I assure you.

We now went on pretty comfortably, and the road, ascending a little hill in a zig-zag manner, we walked up slowly and easily. It was beginning to grow dusk when we arrived at the top of the hill and, after we had gone about half a mile further, our waggons left us and we were obliged to take the wounded as before.

The Cossacks who had guarded us pointed to a fire on the

plain and made signs to us to carry the wounded there. So we set off in about the same order, and in about half an hour we came to the place. One of the Cossacks had rode on in advance and given notice of our coming, and as soon as we reached the spot the wounded were laid down on the ground in a circle round the fire. Those who were unhurt stood up in a second circle round the fire while the Russians formed a solid circle, many deep, all around us. We soon had their officers among us and Mr. Duff was soon in conversation. One of them asked him if we were hungry. He interpreted this to us and we all replied that we were. The Russian officers went away and taking two men with him returned in a short while with several loaves of bread, which he cut into pieces and distributed among us. We enjoyed it very much for it was a great treat. Mr. Duff also came up for his share, but they told him he should have something better. One of them brought a lot of meat and bread and a large flask. Mr. Duff called me to him and gave me some of the bread and meat, and the officer, coming up with the flask, poured out half a tumblerful for Mr. Duff, but he handed it to me and told me to drink the whole as they would be sure to give him some; but the Russian interfered and would have the Capt. drink first, which he did. The officer then filled it for me and wanted to know if I was an officer, and appeared astonished when he found I was but a sergeant.

Mr. Duff now asked them for a doctor to look to the wounded, and we very soon had one, and an assistant who washed the wounds and stuffed them full of what looked like hemp with a little oil on it. He bandaged the wounds and bound them all and through this, I believe, saved many of their lives.

While we were thus standing round the fire I took notice of many of the Russian soldiers eager to bring water, keep up the fire and turn the wounded. Others would slip pieces of black bread into our hands, and some roasted and boiled potatoes, and others apples. Some of them watched their opportunity and, when their officers were not looking, actually kissed some of our men. During the whole of the time we remained there they kept whispering the word 'Polene' in our ears and pointing to themselves. I asked Capt. Duff what they meant, and he told me they were Poles.

No love was lost between the Russians and the Poles. A proud and independent race, they had actually formed an alliance with the Russian Emperor Peter (1689–1725). However, the ruthless and bloodthirsty Catherine the Great (1762–1796), who had deposed her own husband and usurped the throne, had divided the country, and it became an unwilling vassal of St. Petersburg. A rising shortly before the Crimean War had been ruthlessly crushed by Tsar Nicholas. Now the Poles were fighting as conscripts alongside their hated masters, and many deserted to the allies.

We remained here about three hours, when three waggons came for the wounded, and we were told to go before the General. It was now, and had been for some time, quite dark, and we had not gone far before we found that our guide, a Cossack, had lost his way. We roamed about for an hour and a half before we found it, through mud and water and over broken ground, which jolted our wounded terribly, and every fresh jolt would bring a cry of pain from the whole of them. We were wet and dripping mud and water, but at last we found the road and, soon after, the General's tent.

Mr. Duff was called inside, the wounded remained in the waggons, and the unhurt crowded round a bit of fire. Mr. Duff was gone about half an hour and then returned. He told us that this General did not know what to do with us and that we were to go to another. He also told me that there were a great many officers in the tent where he had been, and they owned to him to having got a damn good hiding that day. They treated him kindly, too.

Russian casualties at Inkerman were about 12,000 killed and wounded. British losses amounted to about 2,500 killed and wounded. The return of the losses of the 23rd on that day were: Killed   8
Wounded 22
Missing   14
           —
      44 total.

The other three missing—11 are accounted for by Newman and his party—were taken at the Five Gun Battery.

After about half an hour's march we came to a second General. Mr. Duff again went in and was away about an hour and came back with almost the same story. They had made him have some supper and acknowledged they had got a good drubbing and the General did not know what to do with us. Our men began to complain greatly, for we were all very tired, especially the wounded, but we had no help for it but to go on again.

Another long half hour's march and we arrived at the third General's. Mr. Duff was again taken in and in half an hour returned saying that we had to go back to the North side of Sebastopol, and the wounded would be taken into hospital there.

We had a fresh guard sent with us and the Cossacks left us. We started off back again and kept the greater part of the guard striking lights for our pipes, which they do with a flint and stone and piece of touch-paper. Our men were now so tired that they began to creep up on the edge of the waggons for a ride, where they would soon fall asleep, and several of them rolled inside upon the wounded, eliciting shrieks of pain as often as it happened. After three hours of this doleful march we reached our destination, cold, tired, wet and hungry. By Mr. Duff's orders we lifted the wounded out and carried them inside; but they had no room for them in the wards, so we had to leave them in the small passage on the floor, and we also laid down, but were not allowed to remain long for an old doctor came in and began to kick us up.

"Sacré, got no room here—go," says he, pointing to the door, and outside we had to go, except Mr. Duff who was allowed to stop. As soon as we got into the yard the door was locked to keep us out. We had no other way for it but to snooze in the yard. The night—or rather morning—was raw, cold, and we were wet and hungry, but I took one of the stone steps for a pillow and stretched myself on the ground and was soon fast asleep.

We must have lain and slept here for some hours, but it was still dark when we were awakened by some persons kicking us up and jabbering something that we could not understand, but made signs to us to follow them, and they led us into a room on the other side of the yard. There was not a stick of furniture in it, but it was warm and dry and we were soon on the floor and fast asleep again.

The sun was shining brightly and warmly when we were again roused from our slumbers and turned out of our domicile into the yard. I took the opportunity of taking all the men's names and what regiments they belonged to. In about half an hour Mr. Duff came to bid us adieu. He had been taken out in the town and had learned that we were for the present to be placed in one of the forts, and he was to be taken to more comfortable quarters. I gave him the names of the men and asked him to get them sent into our camp if possible, which he did that evening. He shook hands with the whole of us, and we parted, and I never saw him again until after the exchange of prisoners.

James Duff was born in Elgin in Moray and was 23 at the time of his capture. He had purchased his commission for £500 and joined the regiment on the 15th May 1851. He had been promoted Lieutenant by purchase on the 28th April 1854. On his return from captivity in September 1855 he was promoted Captain and served as ADC to his former Colonel, Col. Lysons, now in command of the Brigade. Lyssons later wrote:

"My Man Friday (Duff) makes a capital ADC, he keeps house and squares the accounts."

He served with the regiment at Cawnpore in 1857 and at the fall of Lucknow in 1858. He was promoted major in 1858.

We were marched between a strong guard to the rear of one of the great forts—which I believe to be Fort Constantine. There was a great crowd to look at us, especially as there was a drummer in front, who kept up a continual roll upon the drum as if to call people's attention to us. I expected they would have shouted or hooted at us, but they did not, they only stared at us and pointed to the lace on our old coatees, and told one another that we were musicians.

Several writers, visiting the Crimea before the war, described the fortifications on the north side, of which the great Fort Constantine was the principle one, guarding the entrance to the Roads. One of the most critical was a French scientist Xavier Hommaire de Hell, who, with his wife, made extensive journeys in Southern Russia in the 1840s. His book, published in English in 1847 was a joint effort by himself and his wife and gives not only a great deal of factual information, but also many graphic descriptions of Russia at this time. Writing of Fort Constantine he says:

"The height above sea level and the three storeys

appear to us to be basically bad. Practical men will agree with us that a hostile squadron might make very light of the three tiers of guns which, when pointed horizontally, could, almost certainly only hit the rigging of the ships.

"The internal arrangements struck as equally at variance with all the rules of military architecture; each storey consists of a suite of rooms opening one into another, and communicating by a small door, with an outer gallery which runs the whole length of the building.

"The improvidence of the Government has been great, for the Imperial Engineers have thought proper to employ small pieces of coarse limestone in the masonry of the three-storied batteries, mounting 250–300 guns. The works have been constructed with so little care, and the dimensions of the walls and arches are so insufficient that it is easy to see, at a glance, that all these batteries must inevitably be shaken to pieces whenever their numerous artillery shall be brought into play."

M. Hommaire's scathing condemnation was to prove totally unfounded in the event. During the bombardment of the 16th October, H.M.S. *Agamemnon* and the British Fleet had caused extensive damage to Fort Constantine, but these were soon repaired, and the fort remained intact.

We were soon at our destination, for we had not far to go, and were placed in a guard room where, to our surprise, we found four English soldiers and four French, taken at Inkerman. Three of the English belonged to my own regiment and were taken at the Five Gun Battery. This re-inforcement made our numbers—English 27, French 7—total 34.

After our long fast we began to feel very hungry, and our men grumbled a good deal that they did not have something to eat. At length some officers came to see us and one of them could talk English pretty fluently and interpreted for the others. They stopped chatting with us for an hour, but at last took their departure, promising to send us plenty of soup and bread, which we were pleased to hear and began to feed our imaginations upon the basins of good soup. But a long time passed and the soup did not make its appearance, and we began to wish the officers all manner of good luck. At length, after waiting full two hours, two men entered—fairly staggering under the weight of a large, deep tub, which they carried on a pole, as our brewers do on their shoulders.

We soon pressed round the tub to see the tasty contents. There was not a sparkle of fat on the top to lead the mind to suppose that there had been meat cooked in it. There was no flour to thicken it or give it consistency, but there were large lumps of cabbage and larger lumps of black bread floating like ships, bottoms upwards. We were all served out a large wooden spoon each and an officer came in to show us how to eat it. By his instructions we were to advance to the tub and fill our spoons and then take two paces backwards, to give the others an opportunity of coming up. As soon as he was done speaking he made his exit, and now there was a general rush to the tub. Such crowding and scalding and cursing and very near fighting to obtain a fair portion of the delicious mess. I was shut out altogether, but I remembered having seen an old wooden dish in a corner that our men had been washing in. I soon possessed myself of this, to me, valuable article and threw the dirty water on the floor. I had nothing to wipe it with, but what did I care for soap suds. I got one of the men, near the tub, to fill it for me and I retired to a corner to pay my best respects to it.

Now our party, being the strongest, had got closest up to the tub from which they would not budge an inch and excluded the poor Frenchmen altogether, who could not get near enough even to see the tub. In vain did they chatter, in vain did they curse, nobody paid the slightest attention to them, nor moved until they could eat no more, by which time there was not a pint left in the large tub for the seven of them. Two of them now wanted to help me, but I would not agree to this, for I was able to finish what I had myself. They went away in a great rage and commenced shaking their fists at me from the far end of the room, at the same time calling me every dirty thing in French until my steam began to get up, but I stopped until I had finished my soup. Then I walked over and told the most forward of them that I would break his neck if he didn't keep silent. Upon this he challenged me to a fight and pulls off his old coat and I mine and we were just about to commence operations when the soldiers of the guard ran in and made signs to put on our coats and turn out.

They were in a tremendous hurry and tried to put on our coats for us as we were in no hurry ourselves. However, we got out at last and were fell in in single rank, with the French on the right.

In about five minutes I noticed two tall, very fine-looking young men coming towards us and several officers following them with their helmets off. They came up and looked at us, and one of them spoke to us in very good English and asked us how we came to be taken prisoner and told us we should be very kindly treated and asked us if we had any complaints to make. We all complained about the black bread, and he sent for some to try it himself. He said it was very good, of the sort, and that their soldiers and sailors were very fond of it.

"But," he says, "I know that you would like better some roast beef and plum pudding, oh! But you shall have white bread in future."

We thanked him, and he passed on to the French and asked if they had any complaints, when the fellow I was going to fight stepped out and made a tremendous complaint against the English for eating all the soup and pointed to me as the principle aggressor. The two Grand Dukes (for such they were, by name Michael and Nicholas) laughed loudly, and so did their staff, as in duty bound. The two Grand Dukes seemed to enjoy it exceedingly and one of them said:

"I will certainly let my father, the Emperor know that the English and French cannot keep the alliance when hungry."

He ordered the French some more soup and then departed. The French got their soup without waiting so long as we did for the other, and they got white bread and much better soup. When they had finished and their hunger was satisfied we were soon friends again, but I could never forgive myself for acting unfairly towards them; but what will not a starving man do?

The two Grand Dukes were the youngest sons of Tsar Nicholas I. Grand Duke Michael, the elder, at 23 Colonel of several regiments, was also Inspector General of the Engineering Department. His brother Nicholas, 22, was also colonel of several regiments, and Quarter-Master General of Artillery.

I may as well mention the name of the Frenchman I was going to fight. He was a remarkable character and I shall have to speak of him again often. His name was Pierre-le-Grand, but we christened him Jack-of-Clubs, from the resemblance he bore to that worthy, and he belonged to the first regiment of Chasseurs de Vincennes. He was as ugly as he possibly could be, and he had but three teeth in the front part of his mouth, which improved his appearance wonderfully.

The first Battalion of Chasseurs à Pied de Vincennes was raised by Royal Ordinance on 14th November 1838. It had served principally in Algeria and at the beginning of the Crimean War it served at Dobrutcha and Alma. It had not been engaged at Inkerman.

Just as it was getting dark the officer who spoke English returned and brought us some tobacco and a large bottle of Walki (a spirit common in Russia). He gave it to me, and this time I saw that it was properly divided among the French as well as ourselves—and I rose in their good graces accordingly. After the Walki, we laid down as best we could and slept soundly until morning.

> The consistent reference to Vodka as 'Walki' is explained by the fact that this is the genitive case of the word and is the way in which it would be most frequently used—e.g. 'Magasin Vodki'—Vodka shop. It will serve to illustrate that Russian names are consistently mispronounced in English. In Sebastopol, for example, the accent is on the last two syllables—'Sebas-topol'.

November 7th.—there was nothing occurred next morning except that they gave us a good haunch of white bread for breakfast, which we enjoyed as a great treat. About twelve o'clock we were told by an officer to get ready to march. I was soon ready, for all I had to do was to fold my lousy greatcoat, which composed the whole of my wardrobe, except what I stood up in; and they would not have fetched fourpence for old rags. About two o'clock we were marched out of the fort. It was a beautiful day and we could plainly see the white canvas tents of our people on the other side, and the flashes from the guns on the different batteries, and we could plainly distinguish the sounds of Lancaster shots as they sped through the air. I wondered to myself how long it would be before I rejoined them—and wished myself among them a thousand times over.

We were marched down towards some houses, which we were told were the Grand Dukes' headquarters. There were two very large travelling carriages standing close to them, which would have taken a dozen horses to each to draw them with speed. We here had a whole crowd round us, and many officers among them, one of whom could speak English remarkably well, I thought. He preached a long yarn to us of the mercy of the Russians in sparing our lives. But some of the men told him they did not thank the Russians a bit for it, as they would much rather have been killed outright than taken prisoner to starve. He looked rather blank at this, but went on to say that if the English should attack the town they would not be so merciful.

"But," he continued, "you will never take the town now— no, never, never. You lost the opportunity, for if you had attacked it the night you came up from Balaclava first, you would have gotten it, for there was not above two thousand men here then; but now we have more than a hundred thousand. No, no," (with a shake of the head and a stamp of the foot), "you will never, never, get it."

"I'll bet you a farthing we do," said one of the men. "You Russians said the same about the heights of Alma," continued the fellow, "but we soon let you know all about it when we did begin."

I could see that Mr. Officer was getting his linen out and I wished to turn the conversation, so I asked him if he was not an Englishman.

"I was once," said he, "but thank God I am now a Russian and not under such d—d laws and government. I would not go back to England if they were to make me a prince."

"And we," said I (for I began to get steam up), "can do damned well without you, and should be all the better if many more of your sort would take a fancy to become Russians."

His monkey was properly up now and he cursed the whole of us and wished our fates were in his hands.

"But," he went on, "you are going to Siberia, and I wish you joy of your journey, for those who go never come back."

As he finished this comforting parting address he stalked

away with great dignity, and I saw him soon after at an open window with one of the Dukes, and I fully expect he misrepresented us to him, for the Dukes did not come to see us as we expected, being so near their quarters.

About half past four we began our march away from the famed town of Sebastopol. We had not gone far before darkness fell, and I found that they were going to march us in the dark, to prevent us seeing too much. The soldiers were very civil, and struck lights for our pipes as often as we wanted them. They would not allow us to wander or straggle outside the escort. We had two waggons to carry our baggage, which could easily have been put in a wheelbarrow, but the waggons were handy to take a rest on while we had a smoke.

At length, about ten o'clock, we came to a place which I thought I remembered. The wide road running down a steep hill with a ravine on one side and the hill above us on the other, the wooden side-rail to the road and the woods all around conspired to make me think we were descending into the Belbec. Nor was I mistaken, for we shortly afterwards came to the village, and I saw the vineyards and orchards that I had such a lot of apples and grapes from when on the march from the Alma to Sebastopol.

Belbec, we found, was the Headquarters of the Russian Commissary, and also a hospital. There was a great many soldiers moving about even at this hour, and we got our share of staring, even in the dark. We passed throught the upper part of the village, past the old Guard House and halted on the road under the hill, which we descended when on our road to Sebastopol. The waggons here left us and we had to climb the hill. About half way up is a flat piece of land, and this was crowded with ammunition waggons. We had a few officers come to look at us and were served out with some black bread and a tot of Walki. We drank the Walki, but held a council of war on the bread, and came to the conclusion that, if we began eating black bread after our complaint to the Dukes, we should always be obliged to eat it. So we determined to leave it alone—although we were tremendous hungry—and try to get white in the morning.

We were each served out with an old corn sack for a bed, and I got a large stone for a pillow. I pulled my old forage cap down over my ears and spread my old greatcoat over me and laid down. I lay for some time watching the stars shoot and thinking of the difference in my fate since I came over this same ground with my regiment—and then wondered how many had been killed at Inkerman, whether my little comrade had escaped or not; but at last I fell asleep.

CHAPTER THREE

Crim Tartary
8th – 18th November

THE RUSSIAN BEAR'S UN-LICKED CUBS,
NICHOLAS AND MICHAEL.

From *Punch*
25th November, 1854

November 8th.—The first thing we did in the morning was to kick up a row about the bread. This we managed to do, by the Frenchmen, to an officer who could speak French. After waiting some time we got plenty of white.

About ten o'clock a soldier brought us a tot of Walki—I dare say there was five or six quarts—and told us the General sent it. We felt much obliged to the General and soon polished it for him.

I began to suffer a great deal from dysentry, and so did all of us more or less. I asked for a doctor and was taken to one directly. I told him I had been passing blood, and he gave me some white powder, but made me stop and talk to him for some time. We were about a match for speaking French, so we got along pretty well together, but he would have me drink Walki, with him counting, and I believe it spoilt the powder he gave me for I was worse afterwards.

When I got back to our fellows I found I was wanted to go to see the General. I was picked because I could speak a little French, and the French sergeant was to go with me; so off we started with an officer and two soldiers. When we came to the place (a hut which had escaped having its roof pulled off when our army marched through) we were received at the door by the staff officers and, as our personal appearance was none of the cleanest, we were conducted to a tub and they gave us some soap and a towel to wash. They seemed rather puzzled that we knew how to proceed with such a job. After we had finished I coolly put the piece of soap in my pocket. They looked as though they meant to take it from me, but they did not, but ushered us into the General's room. We found him lying in bed for he had been wounded at Inkerman.

He was a long, grey-headed, pleasant looking old man. I took a survey of the apartment as we entered. There were two chairs, an old table and the camp bed on which the old gentleman lay. He spoke to me in broken English, bidding me to take a seat, and the same to the Frenchman. His staff officers stood round the room bare-headed, their caps in their hands. The old General spoke first to my companion and I could find that he was a much better hand at French than he was at English. At last he turned to me, and commenced the discourse by asking me if I liked plum pudding and roast beef, adding:

"I'm sure you do, for I never met an Englishman who did not, and you will be able to get plenty up the country when you reach your destination."

He then asked how we had been treated and asked if we were well and told us that we should soon get to a large town where those who were sick could stop. He said something to one of the officers, who went out and soon returned bringing a decanter and some glasses, some biscuits and a large cigar case. He told us to help ourselves, which we did without being told twice.

While we were eating he asked me if the Duke of Cambridge had been at Inkerman and said he hoped he was not hurt, for he knew him well. He then went on to tell me that he lived a great deal in England and that it was a fine country; that he had a country house in Montrose in Scotland and a town house in London. He gave us good advice as to our behaviour in the country and said we were in a very hospitable land and would be treated very kindly, as long as we conducted ourselves well. He also told us that in future we should have daily pay and could buy our own provisions. We stopped with the old gent about an hour and a half, and could not help remarking how easy we took it, smoking and drinking, eating and chatting, while five or six stood all the time at attention with their caps off, while we, dirty, ragged and lousy were sitting at our ease.

The same officer who took us marched us back again, and then told us to get ready to march. We started about four o'clock, with the Frenchmen all about half drunk, for, during our absence, some officers had taken them (the French) away to drink and they had drunk a good quantity and now had a large bottle with them. They were very merry and enlivened our road with their singing and we arrived at Bachtisherai about eleven at night. We could not see much of the town for there were few lamps and the shops were all closed. There was a great smell of fruit as we passed through the streets, and presently we came to a baker's shop with the oven in the shop, and the baker was just drawing a batch and placing it on the shop board for sale the next morning. We had got our pay before we started, at nine copeks per diem (about three halfpence English) so we all made a charge at the baker's shop for hot bread, and made a tolerable good supper of it, for we were very hungry.

Our guard now took us up to some large house—for instructions I think—and then we were marched further down the town and put in a small gaol. We were all put in one large room with a plank bed in the centre and sloping outwards, along the middle, the boards were raised about six inches to form a pillow. We soon took up our quarters and composed ourselves for sleep, for we were very tired and most of us suffering from dysentry; but the Frenchman, still half-seas over, would not be quiet, but continued singing, laughing and chatting, much to our annoyance. We told them we wanted to sleep—expostulated with the sergeant—but all to no purpose. We did not want to fall out with them as they were so few, for we thought it would look cowardly, so we tried again and again to stop them, but without effect. At last Jack-of-Clubs called me a son of a b—h. Flesh and blood could not stand this so I up fist and knocked him down. The little sergeant made a rush at me directly, but I served him the same and some of our men got up and held him off while I polished off Jack-of-Clubs properly. This done they all laid down and we went to sleep quietly.

> Bakshierai was the site of the Palaces of the Tartar Khans of the Crimea, the ruins of which still remain. During the Crimean War it was, with the larger town of Simpheropol, a supply depot for the Russian Army. Describing a visit to Bakshierai at this time H. D. Seymour relates:
> "Upon his now suggesting that we should go to a cook-shop, we willingly proceeded in search of one and were attracted by sundry whiffs, redolent of mutton, to a large corner house where arose a cloud of fragrant steam. Here a number of people were standing in the open street diving into huge projecting cauldrons of soup, from whence they extracted pieces of fat, which they devoured with relish while strolling about among the crowd."

November 9th. Early this morning our prison room and the small yard our windows looked onto were filled with people come to look at the English Lions. There were a great many well-dressed women among them and many of them brought us presents of bread, grapes and tobacco. The French done the best, though, for they had no less than four languages between them; for three of them belonged to the French Foreign Legion—one was a Spaniard, another a Dutchman and the other an Italian, and the Sergeant had a good smother-ing of English. Thus they could hold converse with many, especially in French and Dutch, which are much spoken in Russia. Mr. Jack-of-Clubs was not satisfied with the drubbing I had given him and wanted to have another trial but, as my steam was not up, I would not gratify him.

We were here paid two day's pay, one for the present day

and one for the morrow, and were told to get what we wanted as we went through the town as there was no other places on the road.

We started about ten o'clock with our old guard and two Cossacks, and I was much amused by the dexterity of the Cossacks in stealing for, if they came upon a shop and there was nobody in it, down came their long lances and they would spear what they wanted and it was out of sight in a moment; for the one pushed the point of his lance to the other, who whipped off whatever was on it and concealed it, and they divided the spoil after we had cleared the town.

I had formed an acquaintance and comradeship with a sergeant of the 49th Regiment, and a very good fellow I found him. We laid out our pay as well as we could and, as he did not smoke, I got his allowance of the tobacco that was given. We travelled through pretty country this day and crossed a small river which our guard informed us was the Alma.

The 49th Regiment—the Royal Berkshire Regiment— won considerable distinction at Inkerman. The regiment was on the extreme right of the Second Division. Under Major Grant they had gained an initial advantage when they forced the advancing Russians to retreat towards Shell Hill. Soon, however, a body of enemy, 9,000 strong, attacked and the regiment had to retire. It then became split into two parts; one company under Captain Bellairs joined General Adams before the Sandbag Battery, and Sgt. George Walters won a Victoria Cross for saving the General's life.

Sergeant Surridge, Newman's companion, was to survive the war and was promoted Colour Sergeant on 11th February 1856.

We halted about five o'clock at a prison by the roadside for the night. I may as well add that all the roads I went up the country there were small prisons or guard houses by the roadside where the towns and villages are too far apart for one day's march. They are all built on the same scale: the one floor and two large rooms, one on each hand as you enter, and the space between them is occupied by the guard. The rooms are all furnished the same as the one we left this morning: long sloping plank bed and raised pillow, and all were tremendous dirty—lousy and fleas, but no bugs: I never saw a bug while in Russia.

There was a Walki shop close by, and as we were not allowed to go to it ourselves we got a soldier to go for us and bring us some. My comrade (Sgt. Surridge), having a little money, paid for it. The French again commenced a noise when we wanted to sleep (for they had had some money given to them in the gaol we had left, and were now nearly drunk). They would play at cards and made such a noise over it that we could not get a wink of sleep. We resolved we would not knock them about any more, unless they commenced it. So two or three men went among them and snatched the cards from them and tore them up. They were for fight directly, but our fellows walked back to their places and laid down, and when the Frenchmen had done cursing they laid down to, and we soon got sleep after, but I woke several times through the lice and fleas and had a bad night.

November 10th. We commenced our march at six o'clock this day and had 35 versts to go (a verst is just $\frac{3}{4}$ miles English)

He is wrong about this—a verst is .663 or about $\frac{2}{3}$ of an English mile, i.e 35 versts = about 23 miles.

About eleven o'clock we were overtook on the road by an officer of Cossack, as drunk as glory. He spoke to our guard, and when he found we were English he produced a large leather bottle of Walki and gave it to some of our men, who drank heartily and passed it round, and it was soon empty.

In the meantime he dismounted and proceeded to show us what his horse could do: how he would run after him and stand on his hind legs and put his fore legs round his master's neck as though he was hugging him. When he had done he asked for the bottle and was thunderstruck to find it empty. He jumped on his horse with his face very much elongated and galloped off amid a shout of laughter from our party.

About two o'clock we came in sight of the town of Simpheropol. It is situated on a large level plane and we could see it for a long time before we arrived at it. We passed large herds of cattle grazing on the plain and I heartily wished some of our people had them in our camp.

> Simpheropol, the administrative capital of the Crimea, had a civil population of 8,000, of whom 5,000 were Tartars and 1,700 Russian. The streets were very wide and imposing, although most of the houses were mere whitewashed cottages.

About half past three we entered the outskirts of the town and were conducted to a soldiers' barracks, and the place was immensely thronged by the curious come to have a peep at the English. There was a civilian spoke broken English and told us he was a Polish Interpreter for us and told us we should stop in the town five days and be provided with good warm clothing before we started again.

We stopped for an hour in this place and then fell in and marched off again. I could find we were going to some place of great consequence by the way they made us keep in the ranks and by the soldiers producing old rags and rubbing up their firelocks and ornaments of their caps as they went along. We marched down what appeared to be the main street of the town, and a pretty crowd we had to stare at us, I assure you. At length we stopped before a very large house with a balcony in front, and a large pair of gates were thrown open and we marched into the yard and formed up in front of the door with the French on our left.

A whole host of servants, some of them in livery, flocked out to look at us and presently a good-looking, grey headed old man dressed in rich uniform with lots of crosses and stars on his breast came slowly down the wide steps towards us. He spoke to us in English (but not as well as the Dukes) and enquired how we had been treated and whether our guard was civil and obliging. He then questioned each one in turn as to how he had been taken. He spoke very kindly and told us to behave ourselves and we would be very comfortable. He then asked if we would prefer buying our own victuals while we were in town or to be served out with rations. We answered that we preferred rations if they gave us white bread, as we did not understand the language and were very likely to be cheated.

He replied, "Certainly, certainly you shall have white bread, and if any of you wish to write to your friends I will give you permission and send the letters for you, but you must leave them open for my inspection. And if any of you are ill there are large, good hospitals here—and some of your countrymen in one of them who were taken at the battle of Balaclava."

We thanked him for his kindness and he then went and had a chat with the French (but no complaints about the soup this time). He was now joined by a pretty little boy about three years of age, whom he told to come and shake hands with the English, but the child was afraid and would not come. He then took up the little child and began retiring up the steps and, when half way up, he turned round and said: "Good by, my poor English. May God bless you and send you safe to your wives and mothers."

This man was Prince Menschikoff.

Menschikoff, the Russian Commander-in-Chief, was the great-grandson of Peter the Great's favourite. In his younger years he had been the ruthless trouble-shooter of Tsar Nicholas I, a figure to be feared. Now, at 70, he had been brought from retirement to command the Russian Armies in the Crimea. This picture of a kindly old gentleman, matured by age, is in marked contrast to that usually presented of him at this time.

Private Wightman of the 17th Lancers, who later wrote a short essay on his part in the War, was one of the prisoners in the hospital mentioned by Menschikoff, having been taken at Balaclava. The Grand Dukes had visited him and his party on their way up to the front before Inkerman, and he, like Newman, had complained about the black bread. This apparent obsession with black bread was no mere quibble, Kinglake the historian says that the Russian soldiers paid for white bread themselves. The so-called 'black' bread was so hard that it was quite uneatable unless well soaked in some sort of liquid.

We were now marched off down the same street we came up and were put into a prison where a roll was called and we were told that we should remain five days, with that day included. We had not been long in the prison before I was waited on by Mr. Jack-of-Clubs and the little French sergeant who said that the Frenchmen's wages were very different from ours and that we should always be quarrelling if we stopped in the same room, so he wanted me to go with him to the Governor of the prison and ask to be separated into different rooms. I agreed and off we started and, after some time, persuaded the Governor to allow it, and the French got a little room to themselves on the other side of the yard.

A gentleman brought some tobacco and pipes and flint and distributed it among us and then we lay down on our plank bed and were soon fast asleep.

November 11th. This morning, as soon as we got up—and

that was not early, I assure you—we all set to work to hunt the lice, and such cracking from all parts of the room you never heard. I got to be quite adept at it and could have cracked lice for a wager, either against time or another man. We were in the middle of the sport when the door opened and several gents and ladies were about to enter, but stopped short when they saw many of our party in a state of nudity and so busily engaged among their countrymen. Mind I do not know whether they drew back through modesty or for fear of getting lousy, but I have a poor opinion of their modesty.

As soon as they were gone we made haste and finished our job and got dressed for fear of any more coming, and we soon had some more. Each party as they came brought something for us, such as fruit, bread, pipes, tobacco and some gave us money. We divided all things fairly to each man. Our rations came now and a fine row we had over it. There was about a quarter of a pound of meat per man for the day, a very few potatoes and some onions, with about a pound of bread (good bread) per man. A Russian convict was told off to cook for us and he made a great copper-full of soup out of this allowance of meat. I'll be bound the copper did not hold less that 40 gallons so you can judge the quality by the quantity. At length dinner time came and the soup with it. It was brought up in a tub (like a woman's washing tub in England) and we were provided with spoons (large wooden ones) to commence operations with. You never saw such sport as about a dozen of us standing round a tub diving for the pieces of meat which we were told was in it, but very few found any—I expect Mr. Cook had taken care of No. 1. As for the potatoes, the cook had peeled them and cut them up fine and put them in to thicken the soup. We all professed ourselves highly indignant at such cookery and, the Governor being made aware of it, Mr. Cook was ignominiously dismissed and a young man of the name of McDonell of the 41st Regt. volunteered to cook for us and Jack-of-Clubs for the French, but as we could only eat one meal per diem they had nothing to do that day.

Private Thomas McDonell of the 41st (The Welch) Regiment had only enlisted on 3rd April 1854. He was to return from captivity, but was discharged at Chatham as insane in August 1856. His discharge certificate stated 'Suffered dysentry and fever in the Crimea after which unsoundness of mind appeared.' This probably accounted for the irrational behaviour which Newman records later.

During the day we had many more visitors and among them a Russian officer with his arm in a sling, who told me—through an interpreter (the Pole)—that he had his arm broke by a bullet at the Alma, that he was an artillery officer and was in the redoubt during the whole of the engagement. He was astonished when we told him that we were some of the soldiers who attacked him in the redoubt that day. He gave us a high character for gallantry, said that they never expected we would attempt to climb the bank, and that we rushed up into the battery like a lot of devils. He took great credit to himself for the way they saved their artillery, but I could tell him that they would have lost every piece of it had not some of our officers given a false alarm. He was much pleased to be among us and went to the Governor to let him take some of us to his house for dinner, but it would not be allowed. He asked for permission to bring some Walki in for us, but that also was refused, and he got in a great rage and went away; but one of our men gave him his numbers and grenade out of his cap as a reminder of the regiment who probably broke his arm.

November 12—we took care to be up early and finish our louse hunt before visitors arrived. It was astonishing where they (the lice, I mean) could come from. Though we killed hundreds every morning, yet they were just as numerous or more so on the next.

Two of our men went to hospital this morning with dysentry and, three weeks after, both of them died. I was still very bad, but not so bad as them. Our new cook and Jack-of-Clubs had a fight as soon as they got into the cookhouse about which was to use the copper first, but the governor put a stop to it and gave Jack-of-Clubs an iron pot to cook at and we had the copper. Our soup was better today, for our cook got some flour and made less of it, and the beef and murphies we done separately.

We had some visitors, but the French most, and they done well by them, for they could afford to send out for extra meat and other things, and also got changes of linen—a luxury indeed.

Mr. Jack-of-Clubs here took upon himself the various duties of caterer-cook-treasurer-bully-orator and lover. He bought and cooked everything the French needed; made a long purse out of the leg of a stocking and he compelled the rest of the French to put whatever money was given them into it, and if they grumbled he thrashed them. When any party of visitors came he would leave his cooking and join them, and before he had been three minutes in their company he would have them roaring with laughter, if they understood French. As soon as they were gone he would hurry off to his cooking again, and I several times caught him kissing the Governor's servant girl, who used to cook in the same place, and once, oh dear!—I actually caught him trying to make little Russians. I never came across his equal. This day he nearly strangled the butcher who brought the meat, because he was short in the weight.

We had a little money now that we had had given us, and my mate proposed that we should send one of the guards (a great many more also joined in) for some butter, but what to ask for was the job. We got some of the guard to our room and tried to make them understand by getting a piece of bread and a stick and pretending to spread something on it, but they could make nothing of this notion. So one of our men put on an old sheepskin coat belonging to one of the Russians. Another tied two pieces of stick to his head for horns and another stooped down and pretended to be milking him; another went through the motion of churning and another continued the process of spreading. The Russians laughed loudly at the performance but were as far from the meaning as ever. At last one of them ran into the guard room and brought another soldier, who, after watching our manoeuvres a little, shouted (in German), "Ah, boo-ther, boo-ther," and we were soon able to get some, but the performance took my attention very much at the time.

I took great delight in watching our guard getting their meal (for they had but one meal per day). A large tub of soup— brother to the one we attacked so well in the fort at Sebastopol —was brought in about 2 p.m. Every Russian soldier carries a large wooden spoon for his own especial benefit. The guard assembled round the tub in a circle and proceeded to cross themselves and mumble their prayers. Four men then stepped forward (there is not room enough at the tub for more than four at a time) from different angles of the tub, and took a spoonful and drink it and then fill their spoon again and take two paces backward into their places. They remain eating a lump of black cracker and sipping out of their spoon until their turn comes again, for they go on successively and keep their places well. If any of our party were near while they were eating they would be sure to get a spoon offered them and a place in the circle. After they are done they have another turn at crossing and bowing themselves (which performance we nicknamed copy-catting) and then the sentries are relieved and go to work in the same manner.

November 13. Early rising this morning from off my couch of down; and going into the yard to wash I could plainly hear a terrible cannonading going on at Sebastopol, and we all made sure they were either acting Inkerman over again or that our fleet had got into the mist of the morning, but neither one nor the other was the case and I never heard what was the reason of such heavy firing. This day passed much like the others. We had a few visitors, and Jack-of-Clubs and me got to be great friends and he gave me a sheet of paper that I might write. I expect it was all through my catching him in his wickedness.

In the evening we were told we should march in the morning and the Governor asked us if we would like him to provide some bread for our journey to the next town, saying that for four copecks per diem per man he would provide us with bread, the same quality that we had been eating, for the journey. As the bread was very good, we of course agreed to the proposal.

November 14th. On rising this morning we found the wind blowing a hurricane, accompanied by heavy rain (this was the day that so many of our vessels were lost and the tents blown away in the British camp).

> At Balaclava, the dreadful storm of the 14th of November was quite disastrous to the developing supply problems. Many vital stores and ships were lost including the *Prince*, one of the finest steam ships afloat, having recently arrived with the 46th Regiment and a cargo valued at £500,000.
>
> Colonel Lysons moved the 23rd into the Careening Ravine during the storm, but nonetheless, considerable damage was done to the stores and tents.

I observed, about 7 o'clock several blacksmiths busy at work in one of the rooms rivetting leg-irons on a number of prisoners, and precious large ones they were, too. About ten o'clock we were fell in and marched outside the gates.

We found seven bullock arabas waiting but were allowed only two to put our things in, which was one and a half too many for what we had then got, but we could not make out who the others were for.

By and by the gates opened and out came a host of convicts, all heavily ironed and chained together by cross chains, in fours. Their irons made a great noise and the street was soon crowded with spectators to see the procession move off, although the rain came down very heavily and tiles and chimneys were flying about rather wildly. A soon as Jack-of-Clubs found out we were to march with the convicts his rage knew no bounds; he actually danced with passion. He ran up to the Governor and several officers and told them that the French and English were men of honour, not rogues and thieves, murderers or church robbers; that we were prisoners of war and should be treated as such and marched separately; and concluded by calling them all the bad names in the French tongue and swearing he would write to the Emperor Nicholas about it. If ever he got back with the French army again he would eat the first Russian he came across—a threat that pleased the officers mightily.

At last we moved off, the English leading, the French next and then the convicts with their pleasant music of clanking fetters, and, lastly, the arabas or waggons. Mr. Jack-of-Clubs would not march with the felons and, in spite of the guard, broke from the ranks and got on the path, and all the rest of us followed him and the guard could not get us back again.

We were taken to another prison on the outside of the town, and, after waiting a long time we were served out with a new sheepskin coat each and a pair of new long boots that reached to our knees, and a pair of leather gloves with a piece of cloth inside. While we were waiting we went into a house in the back of the yard out of the wind and the rain. One half of the house was the bakehouse and the other half an office. Here we saw the soldiers paid and we were paid for nine days at 5 copeks per day (four copeks being deducted for bread, and we only got nine copeks per day for a long time after that). While we were waiting the sergeant who had brought us opened a bag and distributed a very small loaf to each of us, telling us to eat. They did not weigh more than half a pound each and, as we were hungry, we soon put them out of sight.

50 copeks was equivalent to about 1/-, so that 5 copeks was a little over one old penny.

The storm outside grew worse and worse and the tiles were flying off the house we were in like mad things, and some of the glass was blown in and the rain and sleet came down very heavily, and the poor, miserable convicts were left in the whole of it.

About four o'clock we were again fell in to begin our march, and were informed that we had about 25 versts to go; a nice job on such a day as this was.

When the gates were opened for us to pass out I saw a crowd of miserable-looking women and children round the entrance, and, though nearly drowned and wet through, I wondered what they wanted; but I soon found out, for as soon as the troop of convicts came in sight they set up an awful cry. Heart-rending it was—I never heard such a cry of lamentation before or since. They rushed in among the convicts in spite of the levelled bayonets of the soldiers, and clung to their knees and hung round their necks weeping and crying most piteously. Now flashed upon my mind what it was all about. These were the wives, children, mothers and sisters of those poor wretches who were being dragged away to the mines of Siberia, from which few, if any, ever return; and they had waited at the gates five long hours in that pitiful storm to take their last farewell of a husband, father, a son or a brother. I never saw such a scene of wretched misery, and God grant that I never do again.

A man now came up on horseback carrying a whip with a long lash. He was dressed as a civilian but must have been some person in authority. He began to make use of the long thong of his whip in a most barbarous manner upon the poor women and children. He elicited shouts of pain at every lash, which he dealt out right and left indiscriminately upon woman or child until he had cleared the whole of them from their unhappy relations, and he then shouted to the soldiers to march on.

As soon as we began to move there was another rush from the poor women upon the convicts, and the whip was applied with renewed vigour and, at last, we got fairly on the move. Poor wretches, my heart bled for them and I thanked God I was not a subject of Russia. Most of them followed us on the road for miles with the most heart-rending cries and often stopping and beating their heads on the ground and chanting some low plaintive song or hymn of distress.

The fellow with the whip often rode back among them to renew his brutal conduct. At last, one by one, they dropped behind. Except one poor woman with a child in her arms who, in spite of the tremendous tempest and the driving snow and cold, strove to overtake us for one more adieu. Every now and then she would lift up the child at arms' length, which the father (such I supposed he was) seeing, would take off his cap and wave it two or three times, which she would answer by a piercing shriek and another effort to come up with us. The fellow with the whip now rode back at her and we guessed easily for what purpose. The whole of our party hooted him as he passed us and my fingers burned to have a rap at him. Down he came upon the poor creature, who dropped on her knees as he came up, with the child upon the ground and her hands clasped upwards. We could see she was begging for mercy, but without effect, for the lash descended again and again until the miserable woman fell forward upon the child, as we all thought, dead. A yell of rage broke from both the English and French, and each one seemed imbued with the same motive, for we all went looking about for stones or sticks and could we have supplied ourselves with either there would have been murder. But there is no stone to be found in this part of the country and very seldom a tree. Jack-of-Clubs was seated on one of the waggons because he did not like walking in the mud with his new boots. The foam was running from his mouth with passion and he applied every invective he could think of on the brute, who now came riding up among us.

We hooted him again, but he only grinned a horrible grin at us in return, but Jack-of-Clubs up with a lump of the soldiers' black bread out of the waggon and threw it at him, striking him on the side of the face. He made a rush at Jack-of-Clubs, the whip uplifted, but Jack stooped and picked up a chain out of the waggon, used to couple the prisoners together, about a yard long with two heavy and curious padlocks at each end. This he whirled round his head and shouted to the Russian to come on, beckoning him with his finger, but the Russian did not seem to relish such an adversary, especially as we had closed round to assist Jack if necessary; so he shouted to the soldiers and pointed Jack out to them, but none of them liked the job so they let him alone. Soon after we saw the brute take a path to the right and we saw him no more.

The storm still continued and our sergeant made signs to us of going to sleep, which we understood as that we were soon going to stop for the night. We had to wade through a river and soon found ourselves in a village where we were billetted by fours and fives on the different peasants' houses, some soldiers going with each party.

As soon as we were got in, one of the soldiers said something to an old man who made some reply, when the soldier up fist and knocked him down. They put us into a room and made a fire of straw in a kind of earthen oven, which soon warmed the room and I observed the mistress (for such I must call her) very busy making some kind of mess in a large pot. I threw my old greatcoat on top of the oven to dry for it was wet through, and I shortly after became aware that there was something burning. I looked at my coat and, to my horror, found that the whole of the shoulder and part of one sleeve was scorched into tinder. This was a bad job for me.

In about an hour the mistress brought in the iron pot and placed it in the middle of the floor and served each of us soldiers, and all with a formidable wooden spoon.

We seated ourselves as do the Turks round the pot and began the assault. It was a kind of macaronney soup—not bad to the taste, and being hot, went down very well. After we had done we lighted our pipes and the old man brought some dry straw and we laid down to sleep, one of the soldiers sitting up for the double purpose of keeping watch and mending old shoes, in which duty he was regularly relieved by the others; for they are all, or very near all, snobs [cobblers].

From this date I have no recollection of the day of the month or even week. Each day passed much like the other, except very small adventures or our arrival at some town.

We started early next morning, for we had to pull up for what we had missed the day before. It was a beautiful day and the sun shone very warm. We had an old sergeant travelling with us to his home, and his wife was with him, an old cross-toothed, ugly woman, but it mattered little to Jack-of-Clubs what she was so that she was a woman. He sat beside her on the waggon holding an old umbrella over her to shade her beautiful skin. He would have his arm round her and would walk with her when she walked, putting her arm through his and strutting like a crow in a gutter; and he would be kissing her, to the great annoyance of her husband, who would get into a boiling rage three or four times a day, to the great amusement of all our party and the evident satisfaction of the old woman.

We were served out with a small loaf each, like the one we had in the prison, from the sergeant of our party, and we found out that Mr. Sergeant had been giving us a feast of our own bread for the march.

As we jogged along we came to a Walki shop by the roadside, and we found a great many Russians there drinking, and we had a glass each; and as I was going away, one of them pulled me back and would have me have another glass at his expense, saying that I was a soldier and a Christian, but, pointing to the convicts, called them Turks, and spit upon the ground (a great method of showing their dislike among the Russians). I had two glasses with him and was very near boosed.

Here let me add that the population about here are nearly all Tartars (called Crimean Tartars, although they extend a long way beyond the Crimea). They are all Mahomedans like the Turks and are greatly disliked by the Russian soldiers. Many of the convicts with us (I was afterwards told) were sent to Siberia for attempting to assist the Allied forces.

We stopped as the night previous in a Tartar peasant's hut, the soldiers turning the whole family out of doors to make room for us, and then making the mistress come back again and make them and us something for supper, and obliging the old man to bring us a lot of straw to lie upon and burn, which he did most unwillingly, and making signs to us when out of sight of the soldiers that he would like to cut their throats.

The next morning we resumed our march, and the manner in which the soldiers procured the waggons was this: the sergeant and some of the men would go round the village and whenever they saw a waggon they would make them bring it, together with somebody to drive it. If the master was away and they had no children big enough to drive, the mistress was obliged to go herself to the end of the day's journey (sometimes 40 versts) and then they were allowed to return, but they got nothing for it but ill-treatment and are liable to be taken the same jaunt again on the morrow if anyone should arrive requiring them. Sometimes we had horses, sometimes bullocks and sometimes dromedaries or buffaloes.

The third day of our march all our bread was gone and we kicked up a fine row about it. At night we arrived at a roadside prison and were cross at being obliged to stop in it as the peasants' huts, though bad, were better than those places, especially as we were sure of some warm supper.

We had not been long in the prison, when a waggon with four horses abreast drove up to the door containing an officer of the French (a prisoner) and a Cossack officer. The French made a complaint to the Cossack officer of the manner in which our bread had disappeared and accused the sergeant of robbing us. The Cossack flew in a great rage and caught the sergeant by the whisker with one hand and thrashed him with the other most unmercifully. I was sorry to see this as I really did not believe the sergeant guilty, as I had frequently seen the soldiers eating white bread when the sergeant was not there.

After the officers had gone the sergeant took his revenge upon one or two of the privates who had been laughing to see him get it. He served them both as the officer had him until he was quite tired with the exercise. The loss of our bread drove us on very short commons for the rest of the march. So much were we hurt by it that we often had to beg and to steal, and, worse luck, we could get nothing but black bread by either action, for white bread is only to be come by in the towns.

Our day's work after the march consisted of an hour and a half's wholesale slaughter of lice, for which purpose we had to strip naked each night. After lousing we had a wash in the best manner possible and then we would start off begging and if we got the opportunity, stealing, for we did not understand starving. In these rounds through the village we were generally accompanied by one or more soldiers, who used to go snacks [shares] when we got home and started the eating business.

One comfort was that our stock of tobacco was pretty large

and we could smoke as much as we wanted. We did not now march as before, surrounded by the escort, but would walk in front for miles, sometimes getting to our village of rest three or four hours before the convicts, waggons and guards. This we continued to do the whole journey, and I assure you it was a relief to get away from the clanking of the irons.

CHAPTER FOUR

Into Russia
18th November – 25th December

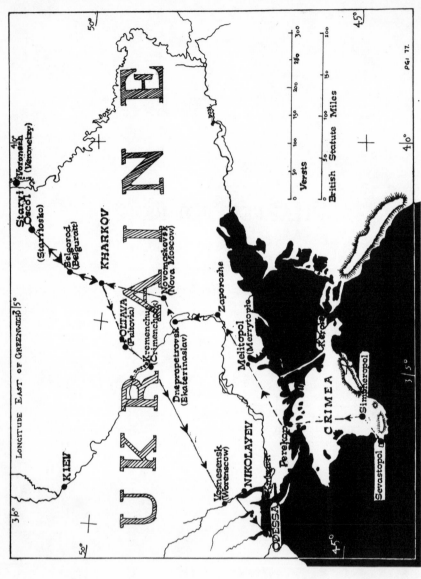

THE TRAVELS
OF THE
BRITISH
PRISONERS
OF WAR

Thus passed the time until we came to the town of Perekop, the old and the new. We halted in the first we came to (the old) and were not placed in a prison but billeted on the inhabitants. I with some more were billeted with a German tailor and we took possession of his principle room. It was a pretty large, comfortable-looking place with several looking-glasses round the walls, and pictures, and an old fashioned case clock and two or three tables and a dozen of chairs; besides which the windows (in themselves a luxury) had blue curtains and the floor, though of earth, was clean. It put me in mind of home to see such things, but yet we were miserable while there, for we did not like to strip to hunt lice in such a fine place, so we were obliged to let them have a holiday, which they did not forget to use to advantage, for the room was warm and I could feel them having a regular field day about my body.

We slept on the floor but had no straw. We expected to march next day but we did not do as the day was very wet, and about ten o'clock a man called and paid us three days' pay, which set us on our legs once more. We were allowed to go to the market but had some soldiers with us. I went for my comrade (Surridge). We met some Cossack officers in the market who could speak French and I was brought up to the front to parly. He spoke French too well for me, but I kept on answering his questions as well as I could, and when he had finished he gave me two roubles, which we marketeers divided among us. I brought two sheep's plucks (heart, liver and lungs) and a good stock of bread and onions, some tobacco, soap, needles and thread and a Russian comb, about the size of a mane comb, with a small tooth louse trap at the back.

Me and my mate had a great feed of liver and lights and heart that day, I assure you, and we clubbed together and bought a pack of cards for amusement. I had a fight here as to who was the first for cooking, but we were separated after a couple of rounds and I got the worst of it.

The next morning we started off again and were first taken to the prison where the convicts had been kept during our stay. We here received eleven days' pay more, all in copper and as I carried away the money for my mate and me I found it very heavy.

We then marched for new Perekop—a distance about 4 miles—and a dreadful dirty place it is; the sludge in the streets was up to our knees. We passed through the main street, a long, wide street with plenty of shops on either side. We here set to work to lay in a stock for the road, and I bought as much bread as I could tie in one of our old greatcoats. After I had bought the bread we went in search of some salt, and seeing a large loaf that took my fancy, I bought it. I then went to a chemist's shop for salt, and while being served I laid the loaf on the counter. I got my salt and paid for it and walked out of the shop, and left my fine loaf behind, and did not remember it until we were four or five versts from the town, a sad loss on my part.

As we came into this town we could see the blue water on our right and left, so it must have been situated on the isthmus. We also crossed over a bridge (a wooden one) thrown across a very deep cutting, as deep as many of the cuttings on a railway. Many of our men would have it that it was intended for a fortification, as the dirt had been thrown up all on one side, but I think it was an unfinished canal, meant to join the sea of Assoff with the Black Sea at this point, but it had never been finished.

Newman's companions were right. The ditch was built

originally in the fifteenth century by the Tartar Khans of the Crimea and was defended by a stone wall with towers. It had been improved in 1736 to make it 72 ft. wide and 42 ft. deep. Seymour describes it in 1853:

"At the present time there is a bridge across the Fosse and a stone gateway, which presents rather an interesting appearance. On either side are a few straggling houses inhabited by Jews, Tartars and Russians. The principal part of the town is at a distance of about two miles and goes by the name of Armenian Bazaar. It contains a custom house and compounds for the brandy distilleries and salt magazines; a number of shops and 900 inhabitants. The quantity of salt is immense."

We had fifteen more versts to march this day and we left Perekop about one o'clock, and now we were in Russian Tartary. The country round about for hundreds of miles is a complete level, not a hill to be seen anywhere, nor a tree nor a bush nor a stone. One large, dreary plain overgrown with tall weeds from which we often started hares, but more often, herons, who would allow us to come quite close to them before they would take wing. When on the main road we could see before and behind us one long line of verst posts as far as the eye could reach and as straight as an arrow, but appearing to get shorter as they merged upon the horizon. Sometimes we came across large herds of cattle grazing with no person to guard them, and often we came across the carcasses of horses who had died on the road, and broken waggons.

Sometimes we would be enlivened by a carriage coming up, drawn by six or eight horses abreast, and we could always see them coming, at first as a small speck in the distance and gradually becoming more defined. When they came up they would stop and have a chat, and Jack-of-Clubs was always on the lookout and many a rouble he and the French got from travellers. We also often met large trains of ammunition waggons, all painted a bright green with several white flags on the tops of the waggons to give notice of danger, and our guard would always want us to put out our pipes as soon as ever they came in sight, although several versts away. We also met with several regiments on their way to Sebastopol, and when we did we always had a short halt and a chat with those who could understand us; but by this time we had managed to pick up a good bit of Russian and some of our men could jabber away first rate.

Sgt. Major Gowing of the 7th Fusiliers wrote, in October 1855:

"The exchange of prisoners had taken place and some of our men, who had been in Russian hands for upwards of twelve months, proved themselves very useful as interpreters."

We suffered a great deal from the heat of the sun some days, and the great scarcity of water. I recollect one hot day when we we were all very dry, we could catch a glimpse of water before us and we pushed on in haste to reach it. I was the first one at it, for I was always considered a good walker. I knelt upon the shores of a pretty large lake and stooped my head for a drink when, to my surprise and disappointment, I found that the water was salt and the whole shore was covered with pieces of rock salt as large as walnuts. For days after, all the water we could get was brackish, and some of it so bad we could not cook with it but had to go and skim up water in hollow places, which had drained there or had remained there from the last rain.

These salt lakes around Perekop formed, as quoted by Seymour earlier, an important part of the local economy. The waters were also claimed to have remedial powers, and sufferers were encouraged to bathe in these putrid waters to cure all manner of ills.

Another thing that attracted my attention greatly was many large mounds of earth thrown up at some time, but now overgrown, like the rest of the plain, with weeds. They appeared to be at long but equal distances apart and I could never make out what they were intended for.

These ancient mounds, at from one to three versts distance, were erected by the roving lords who had inhabited the plains in the seventeenth and eighteenth centuries. They were beacons, used both as a warning of approaching danger and to show the way.

One day we came upon a fine lot of mushrooms and for miles that day we continued to pick them. Me and Surridge had one of our greatcoats full of beauties, and that evening we bought some veal and stewed it with all those mushrooms. The liquor was as black as ink, but we polished it off with great gusto and didn't I have diarrhoea bad next day.

There is another circumstance I must not omit that happened during this march. We arrived at our halting place one night and were billeted as usual and proceeded to our diversion of louse hunting, when I noticed the Tartar mistress of the house going to wash her child (a boy) and called attention of the method to the others. But first I must inform you that both the Russians and Tartars have a curious cradle for their children. It is a square frame with a piece of canvas covering the bottom. It has a cord from each corner joined in a loop above, to which is made fast a long cord, and then passed through a staple in one of the rafters. The child's bed is made in this frame and he is put in and generally left in the whole day. If he gets cross and cries they merely give the frame a sharp push and set the youngster swinging all over the house. Of course, as they don't take him out, the youngster has to do the wants of nature where he is and then wallow in it, until his gentle mother thinks proper to take him out and clean him. By the side of the fire on the hearth is always an earthen pot standing. It somewhat resembles a coffee pot, but the spout is much longer and curved. This pot is always kept full of water and generally used for drinking, but on this occasion it was used for another purpose.

The mother took the child out of its bed of old rags and pieces of old sheep skin and stripped the youngster naked, and you may rely on it he was in a mess. He was completely covered with 'gold dust'. She took hold of him by his ankles and then, taking a mouthful of water from the pot commenced squirting on him, commencing at his feet; thus all the 'gold dust' was carried by the water completely over the youngster head and face and ran up his nostrils. He did not appear to fancy the scent though, for he roared lustily. A bad job for him, for now he got it in his mouth, but the mother took no notice of his squalling but continued the operation, applying herself to the pot of water and then squirting it on him until the child was not only half smothered but half drowned as well. The operation pleased us mightily and we gave the old woman a cheer when she had finished.

Our stock of bread now began to run short, and I caught one of our guard stealing it when he believed we were all asleep. We now began to hunt about for some other cheap food to eat when we got in at night and in the morning, before we started; and one of the men having stumbled on some very coarse oatmeal, we determined to have 'stir-about'. The meal was very cheap and we generally managed to get some milk or butter to eat with it. As I was a good hand at Stir-about I was elected Cook Extraordinary and got my name up greatly as a man of 'taste'. I used to have to carry the stir-about stick (a stick made for the purpose, about the size of a rolling-pin) as my baton of office, and really it made fine wholesome food and cured many of our men of diarrhoea and made me much better than I had been for months before.

At length, on arriving at our halting place one evening, the convicts were so terribly knocked up (for we had had a long march that day) it was determined to give them a rest all the day following. That evening passed as usual but, early on the next morning I and several others were out on the forage for provisions when we were hailed in English by a parcel of men dressed in sailors' rough coats and, some of them, south-westers. On going up to them we found that there was the whole crew of a transport ship called the Culloden, which had been ship-wrecked on the 14th of November, during the heavy gale, and taken prisoners. They had about 100 Turkish soldiers on board at the time, who were also taken prisoners and marching with them. The captain had been sent to Sebastopol, but the chief mate and second mate were with them.

It appeared that their vessel was so much distressed during the night that they were obliged to cut away the masts, and she afterwards drove to within five hundred yards of the shore, where she struck and stuck fast. The crew made sure of being rescued by some of the Men-of-War the next morning as they were so close to Sebastopol as to be able to see the flashes of the guns; but when morning came there was no sign of assistance, and the sea rolled so heavily, although the wind had dropped, that the boat could not live in the water. To their astonishment, in about an hour afterwards, large bodies of troops were seen on the banks of the shore, and soon after a battery of field pieces was brought to the spot and commenced sending them polite invitations to come on shore, in the shape of 24 pound shot (for the Russians have very heavy artillery). Our sailors thought it was best to keep out of sight as they could not return the compliment, but Johnny Russian put a few of his pills into the old ship and seemed as though he was determined to knock her to pieces; so they held a council of war and agreed to go on deck and try to get the long boat overboard: a very difficult task as they had no masts or tackling to lift her with, so they had to cut away the bulwarks and slide her overboard, and trust to providence for her sinking or swimming, but she swam. And now they had a row as to where they should go. Some were for pulling out to sea and chancing being hit; others for going ashore, as they felt certain they would not escape the shot of the enemy, little short of a miracle; and then the sea was so rough that ten chances to one but they were swamped; and if not—the heavy sea rolling would keep them within range of the battery of field pieces so long that they would be sure of being hit. They could not agree, however, upon their route; but they all, with the exception of one, got their bags of clothes and plenty of provisions into the boat. They then got in themselves and again commenced to argue the point as to the route; but Johnny Russ put a spoke in the wheel that decided the matter quickly: for, seeing them in the boat, he let a shower of grape fly at them, which knocked up the water all round them.

The captain then said that if they left the shelter of the ship they would be cut to pieces by the grape, and their only chance was to get on shore. The enemy obliged them with a little more grape shot to add weight to his remarks, and then the captain ordered a white flag to be shewn and the firing ceased. The captain then got some volunteers to pull him ashore in one of the small boats at the risk of being upset, and went to see what terms he could make for the rest, and he was to wave a handkerchief if all was right.

In a short time the signal was given and they went ashore, and in the evening, when the sea had gone down, the Russians prevailed on the sailors to go and fetch the Turks off, among whom were some killed and wounded. They had travelled from thence to Perekop and left at one day after our party and had arrived in this village early this morning, for they travelled much quicker than us, having a waggon and two horses for each two, and no convicts with them. They were not paid as we were, but they had a Cossack officer in charge of them, who took their money and found them food during their journey. They were much pleased at meeting with us, and we with them. They were to have a rest day like us on the following day, and we wanted them to forego it and come with us, but it would not be allowed, and so they continued, one day's march in rear of us, for some time.

It has been impossible to trace a *Culloden* in the transports in the Crimea. For administrative purposes, the smaller ones were given numbers during the war making identification difficult. Transports number 20, 31, 57, 89, 1, 5 and 6, all small brigs, were wrecked on the beach during the storm, and Cossacks came down and took one or two of the crews prisoner.

This evening, on searching my old woollen guernsey as usual, I found it to be so full of lice that I determined to throw it away, which I did. I did not miss it during the night, for the room was very warm, but next day we had 44 versts to march and it began raining just as we started and continued the whole day, heavily. We were all soaked to the skin before we had finished one half of the journey and our sheepskins and greatcoats were in the same pickle, so we had nothing to lie down on during the night. I expected a fine cold through this, especially in leaving off my old guernsey, but I comforted myself with the reflection that the rain, which would cause it, had drowned a few hundred lice for me; but I never felt any ill effects through it.

During the next day's march we spread our sheepskins on top of the waggon in the sun and soon got them dry again. In the afternoon, as we marched along we were overtaken by a Cossack officer, who drove along slowly with us for some time to talk to us, but as he could speak nothing but Russian we could not make out much of what he said.

We came upon a drove of sheep grazing with no one to watch them except two or three dogs. He made signs to us to take two and cut their throats and divide them among us. He said something to the soldiers and two of them started off with several of our men and Jack-of-Clubs towards the living mutton; but the dogs shewed fight, upon which one of the guard put a cartridge in his piece and fired at one of them, who went off limping with a broken leg and followed by the others. Jack-of-Clubs now pointed out two of the flock who were soon secured by the soldiers and Jack cut their weasands [throats] in a complete butcher-like fashion.

The officer now rode on and thought it a fine way to be benevolent at a cheap rate. I have since heard that the officer in charge of the sailors got the meat in precisely the same manner, and, of course, put the sailors' and Turks' rhino [money] to his own use; but I believe he gave them plenty of it, as well he might, when it cost so little; but they only come this dodge in Tartary, for it would not answer in Russia proper.

The poor Tartars have a miserable time of it and often they have made signs to us that they would like to cut the guards' throats.

For some distance coming through Tartary a few of us were planning our escape by securing the arms of the guard, which they left standing about anyhow, and marching them as prisoners to the seaside and getting ourselves and them aboard some British or French ship; but the difficulty lay in being sure we should find a vessel when we got there and how we were to manage to escape the Cossacks, who guard the coast. But, although the thing was often spoken of, yet, as we had not the certainty of finding a ship, we did not attempt it. I feel certain that the Tartars would have assisted us, but perhaps it was all for the best that we did not attempt it, for we might have run right into some of the bodies of troops marching down to Sebastopol.

The Tartars always behaved very kind to us, often refusing to take money for their goods, and in one very large village we passed through, the women and girls ran to us with dishes of different kinds of food, but not much suited to an English palate, while an old man, remarkably well-dressed for a Tartar, stood in the road and gave each a small piece of silver as we passed.

At length, one evening our guard informed us that we should be in a Russian village next day and that we should see no more Tartars (convicts excepted). As we came near to the village we could distinguish the dome and cross of the church, the dome being painted bright green. The houses also looked better (although they were bad enough) for the roofs were higher and they were larger and some of the houses even had glass windows.

We found here that the guard could not shove us into any house they thought proper, but there was a regular Billet Master here, who told us off to our respective lodgings. I and three others (my comrade Surridge among them, of course) were billeted in a miserable hovel, every way unlike the rest of the village. It appeared to me that the founder had been trying to build a house without materials, for it was nothing but a large square hole dug in the soft black mould (which in this countryside is a great depth) and roofed with a few old boughs and plenty of earth and sods. We had to descend into a pretty deep hole to get to the door of our noble mansion, and inside I saw that they had been obliged to secure the roof by ungainly, but strong, props. I expect there was a pretty weight on them after a good shower of rain.

Trumpeter Farquharson of the 4th Light Dragoons also describes this method of construction: "Here and there, over an extent of ground, we saw smoke as it were slowly rising out of the ground. It turned out that we had lighted upon a locality where the people lived like moles, burrowing in the ground. They commence the construction of their habitations by digging a large hole, in a slanting direction. To right and left of this passage, as one may call it, they cut out chambers, the roofs of which are supported by wooden planks. The chimney is formed by boring a hole in the roof upwards to the outer air. One or two of the better off of these earth dwellers sported a chimney-pot over the hole."

We found, upon entering, a middle-aged woman spinning at an old-fashioned wheel, and a very old woman lying on the floor on an old sheepskin coat. She was apparently done up and kept on making a low mournful sound and waving her skinny arm in the air. The other woman never moved when we came in, but looked at us very hard. We began to ask her for milk and other things that we wanted, but all we could get from her was, 'I have none'. At last we asked her for fire, and with like success, and we began to wish ourselves among the Tartars again. I felt a great many things running up my legs and presently after saw the woman at the wheel leave off spinning and deliberately put her hands under the old rag she wore as a pettycoat and pull it out again and rub something between her fingers and then place it between her thumb nail and her fingers and crack it. This was enough for us and we picked up our traps and returned into the open and sweet air, but we carried a little armful of fleas with us, for which they were very grateful.

The member of Parliament, H. D. Seymour, who had

travelled extensively in this area had written: "The houses of the Tartars, even the cottages of the poor are extremely clean, being often white-washed. The floor is generally of earth, but smooth, firm and dry and covered with mats and carpets. With so much cleanliness it is surprising to find the itch prevalent. It is also difficult to escape venomous insects and vermin. The tarantula, scorpion, cockroach, lice, bugs, fleas, flies and ants are more or less prevalent everywhere."

When we got in the road we saw some of our men in a house close by where there was a great noise going on inside. We went to the place and found it to be inhabited by three ladies of easy morals, and about a dozen of our men were there, so we joined them. There was also a great part of the guard, including the sergeant. We found that Walki was the only thing to be got, so we had some. The ladies entertained us to several dances to the tune of an old accordion, which one of them had in her hand while the others footed it merrily. It was amusing to see their attempts at agility with a large pair of boots on which reached to their knees.

There was some pretty goings on that night, but I will not attempt to describe it. In the morning I picked myself up, very ill, from under one of the benches that ran round the wall. One of my own regiment accused me of robbing him of money, which I firmly denied. Compliments passed and I gave him an ear-oler, and then we had a battle royal, to the edification of the Russians, ladies and gentlemen, and I came off victorious and without a scratch.

Just after the fight the ladies disappeared and one of the men told me he had discovered a tub of pickled cabbage in their bedroom. So three or four of us went to have a treat. We found the sleeping apartment of the modest, fair ones quite dark, and while one was trying to knock up a light, the rest of us groped about for the tub, and found it. As soon as it was found I got my hands into it and could feel it was cabbage and cut up in the manner that we cut up cabbage for pickling. So, without hesitation I crammed some of it into my mouth, but, by the Lord Harry! I never tasted anything so nasty in my life. It served me in lieu of an enema, for I nearly threw my heart up.

When we got a light we proceeded to inspect the apartment and found the beds were little berths, like ships' berths, one above another. There was six of them and each of them had a kind of straw palliass and old sheepskin coats for bedclothes; but the ladies returned and caught us in their bower, but did not seem in the least surprised, but invited us to have a snooze, which I, of course, gratefully declined.

About ten o'clock we got on the move again and now we found the country a little pleasanter, for we had a few trees and hills to look at and now and then a tidy-looking home. In the afternoon I was far in front of the convoy and came up to a very large house built of red bricks and had a fine pair of gates. There was a young man at the gate, very well dressed, who, when I came up, said something in Russian I did not understand; and he, seeing it, spoke in French and asked me what I was; and when I told him I was an English prisoner of war he invited me into the house where I was introduced to a young lady and two older ones, and was soon jabbering as well as I could with the younger one. She was a pretty girl and presently asked me to have something to drink, to which I did not demur in the least, and soon found myself paying respects to some stewed mutton and roast Turkey, washing it down with some good walki. At last the convoy came up and I was obliged to leave them.

We now descended a steep hill into a large town and were lodged in the prison. We here found two cavalry who had been taken at Balaclava. One belonged to the 4th Light

Dragoons and the other to the 8th Hussars. They had been left in hospital and their party had gone on.

We found a new dodge for killing lice, which was to put our clothes into a warm oven; but some of our men made the oven too hot and burnt their old rags greatly. We were not allowed to walk out in the town except to market once a day under an escort. We stopped here two or three days, and the cavalry men told us they were receiving twenty copeks per day since Simpheropol and that, if we stuck out, we should get it too. I told the Frenchmen, and Jack-of-Clubs in his glory, going from one to the other, telling them not to march without we got twenty copeks per day.

On the morning of the day of our departure two officers and a clerk came to pay us. Jack-of-Clubs was to receive the money for the French and I was to receive it for the English. Jack got served first—counted it and gave it back and told them it was the Emperor's orders to give us 20 copeks per day. In vain did the officer argue the point and persuade Jack-of-Clubs to take it. He would have nothing to do with it unless they gave him at the rate of 20 copeks per day. They then turned to me, but I stood fast and demanded the same as Jack. They now paid the cavalry men, who were to march with us, at the rate of 20 copeks, and we were determined to have it, too.

They now ordered us to march, and we saw them give it to the sergeant to pay us when we got on the road; but this would not do at any price as doubtless we should have lost the greater part of it. So we refused to leave the prison unless our demands were satisfied (only think of prisoners of war making their own terms). They now sent for some other person, who upon his arrival we found to be a grey-headed, old officer, and he appeared to be the highest in authority. He enquired into the circumstances and then wanted to know what the English would do with their prisoners if they turned mutinous and refused to march when ordered or take the money, when offered, for their support.

We argued the matter with him a long time, and at last compromised the matter by signing a paper for us to get it at the next town we came to, the sergeant of the escort taking charge of the paper. As we passed through the town we bought our stock of provisions and fell in with some of the sailors again, who had come into the town the day after us and were to march next day. The town, I now recollect, was called Merrytopol, and we were told that the next town on our route was called Alexander.

> Melitopol is about 200 miles from Sebastopol and was the trading centre for the extensive German colonies in the area. The scenery around is very desolate, the ground often covered with innumerable fossils.
>
> The former fortress of Alexandrovsk lies just over a mile south of the Dnieper river, about fifteen miles north of Melitopol.

I forget how many days march we had before we reached Alexander, but the time passed much as usual. Jack-of-Clubs, whenever we entered a village used to pull and maul all the girls he could get hold of, to the amusement of the whole lookers-on, of whom we always had plenty on our arrival in each village; and the guard, who liked the fun, would catch and hold the girls for Jack-of-Clubs to kiss them, and when any of the men spectators did not like it and showed symptoms of being jealous, they were pretty certain of getting a quitting from one of the guard.

One day we arrived at our destination and I was particularly struck by a large good-looking house with red tiles and altogether having the appearance of an English country gentlemen's house. There was a nice garden all round it and a gravel road with a green gate and palings. We were soon all collected viewing the curiosity when some well-dressed people came out and asked if we could speak Dutch. The Frenchmen soon brought their Dutchman up to the front and there was a great deal of talking ensued, but they gave nothing to him, much to the disappointment of Jack-of-Clubs, who stood by ready to take it from the Dutchman as soon as given.

At last we all separated and went to our billets, and I had just commenced concocting a large mess of stir-about for nine hungry fellows besides myself, when in came a tolerably well-dressed servant carrying a large basket of mutton and vegetables. He counted us and then left us a good quantity of both. Of course, the stir-about was ignominiously ejected and all hands were soon busy getting a better supper ready. After it was cooked and we were just going to begin when in came a fellow of my regiment, drunk, and threatened to kick over the whole. We tried to induce him to go quietly to his own billet, but he would not go and commenced abusing me and kept it up until I could stand it no longer, so I gave him a topper, and we set to work and I gave him a good trimming and got him out of the house. We then sat down to our supper and had nearly finished when in he came again, stripped to his skin, and would have another hand in. Of course, I obliged him and basted him once more, and two of the men took him forcibly to his own billet, and we saw no more of him that night. The next morning he cut a pretty figure, for his face was terribly cut.

There was nothing else occurred on our march to Alexander, which we reached on a Sunday and were put into a prison were we amused ourselves by card-playing, singing, lice hunting and mending our old rags. You would scarce believe the superiority of the French soldiers' clothing over our own, for while ours were all rags and tatters, theirs were good, strong, whole and always looked tidy.

We stopped two days at Alexander and then went for our

pay to proceed onwards, and fully expected the 20 copeks per day according to the agreement, but could not get it. We did not kick up a row about it here, but were assured that we should get it at the next town.

Alexander is a tremendous dirty place, the sludge in the streets was knee deep and the prison was awful through filth, lice and stench. I never wish to see such an abominable place again.

The first day of our march from Alexander we crossed the river Dnieper in large, flat-bottomed barges which carried the bullocks, waggons and ourselves. On the other side was a pretty Dutch village where we were billeted for the night, and very proud they seemed to have us. The houses were built well, very clean and comfortable. Large cowsheds, well stocked with good-looking cows, were attached to each house, and large stacks of hay and corn neatly thatched made the place look very comfortable and homely.

The German (not Dutch) colonies had been established in 1784 by Catherine the Great to colonise, farm and bring some sort of prosperity to the region formerly occupied by the Zaporogue Cossacks. The colonists were members of the strict Christian sect, the Menonites.

In 1854 there were 16 of these colonies and about 4,250 inhabitants. Madame Hommaire graphically describes them:

"The region occupied by these colonies is unlike the steppes, though the form of the ground is the same. The villages, very close to each other, are all built on the same plan, and are for the most part sheltered in ravines. The houses have only a ground floor and are built with wood or red and blue bricks. Their party-coloured walls, their carved wooden chimneys and pretty straw roofs, which seem as neatly finished as the finest Egyptian mats, produce a charming effect as seen through the green trees of the gardens which surround them. They are almost all exactly similar, even to the most minute details.

"The fields are in excellent cultivation, the pastures are stocked with fine cattle and sheepfolds, and wells, placed here and there, enliven the landscape; the whole face of the country tells of the thriving labours of the colonists. But one must enter their houses to appreciate the habits of order and industry to which they owe not only an ample supply of the necessaries of this life but almost always a degree of comfort rarely to be found in the dwellings of the Russian nobles. One might even accuse the good housewife of a little sensuality, to see their eider-beds and pillows heaped almost up to the ceiling. You may be certain of finding in every house a handsome porcelain stove, a glazed cupboard containing crockery and often plate, furniture carefully scrubbed and polished, curtains to the windows and flowers in every direction."

On going into one of the houses we commenced trying to bargain for some victuals, but soon found that they had already started cooking for us. We were put in a nice little room with the floor as white as milk, and adorned with tables, chairs and a sofa, and pictures on the walls and an old-fashioned clock and many other things indicative of comfort. As soon as supper was ready we sat down to table in comfort, for we had not seen such a place for a long time. Our supper consisted of bacon and spuds, and very good it was. After supper the whole family came into the room and tried to talk with us. Our language is very much like theirs and they would laugh and seem pleased when we called anything the same, or nearly the same as themselves. The master brought a book and made signs to us to write our names and regiments in it, which we did. He then asked for one of our buttons each, which we gave him and he appeared much pleased. The children now commenced to chalk small sums on the table, and the whole of them seemed astonished to find that we understood it. Then they brought Bibles and prayer books and were pleased when we knew what they were. They covered the floor with straw and gave us some rugs and we had a comfortable night's snooze, but were afraid of making their place lousy, especially as we could not have a lice hunt when we first came in.

The next morning we had a good wash and after a good breakfast of bacon, potatoes and milk and bread we started off on the road again. I found out that these Germans have great privileges under the Russians. They pay no tax and are all free men, their children are not liable to be called upon for soldiers, and they are not obliged to find conveyance for baggage, troops or felons, like the Russian serfs.

After the middle of the day we came to a village, and a well-dressed man stood outside a Walki shop with several people and buckets full of Walki, which they distributed among us, the consequence of which was a glorious flare-up. After the Walki the whole of us pushed on a long way ahead of the escort and got to our destination that day a long time before the waggons and guard came up.

On starting the next morning our heads were none of the clearest and we were rather dull until we reached a Walki shop, where we each had a reviver and proceeded on in much better humour and were given to understand by the guard that we should soon come to a nobleman's house—and one of the greatest importance, it appeared from the manner in which they told us; for they seemed afraid even to speak above a whisper, while we, to show our independence of any nobleman, commenced singing and shouting. We soon came to a low wooden fence enclosing a kind of park, and, after some time, came in front of what in summer must have been a very nice garden with a low, large house in the centre.

Madam Hommaire describes just such an estate:

"There is one thing indicative of princely sumptousness, namely, an immense garden which almost makes one forget the steppes, so thick is the foliage of its beautiful alleys. One is at a loss to conceive by what miracle this park, with its large trees, its fine fruit and its charming walks, can have thus sprung up out of the scorched and arid soil, that waits whole months for a few drops of water to clothe it in transient verdure. And, indeed, to create such an oasis in the heart of so barren a land there needed not one miracle, but a series of miracles of perserverance, toil and resolution, seconded by all the means at the disposal of a Russian lord. All kinds of fruit are here collected together; we counted more than fifty varieties of pear in one alley. Grapes of all kinds, strawberries, beds of asparagus of incomparable flavour, everything in short that the most capricious taste can desire grows there in such abundance, that seeing all these things one really feels transported into regions the most favoured by nature.

"No one but a Russian lord could have affected such metamorphoses. Master of a whole population of slaves, he has never to pay for labour; and whims which would be ruinous to others cost him only the trouble of conceiving them. In the dry season, which often lasts for five months, chain pumps worked by horses supply water to every part of this extensive garden, and thus affords what the unkind skies deny it. The work to be done in the spring generally requires the labour of more than 200 pairs of hands daily and during the rest of the year three score peasants are constantly employed in pruning the trees, plucking up the weeds that rapidly spring up in the walks, training the vines, and attending to the flowers. In return for all this expenditure the lord has the satisfaction of seeing his table covered with the finest fruits and most exquisite preserves; and for one who inhabits a desert these things unquestionably have their value. On the whole it is a real 'pays de cocagne' for good cheer. The steppes abound with game from grouse to the majestic bustard. A hunter is attached to the farm and daily supplies the table with all the delicacies of this sort which the country affords. It is evident, therefore, that in a gastronomic point of view it would be difficult to find a more advantageous residence."

I was in the middle of that popular song 'Hurrah for the Road' and a dozen of the others shouting the chorus (to the evident dismay of the guard) when a grey-headed old gentleman with two young ladies looked over the fence.

Published in 1835 the song 'The Road, The Road' from the opera 'Paul Clifford' by Rodwell and Fitzball contains the line 'Hurrah for the Road'.

The whole of the guard immediately uncovered and we stopped our noise. The old gent asked who we were and was soon told we were English prisoners. He appeared astonished at the news and so did the ladies and asked if anyone could speak French. It so happened that the French were some distance in the rear, and so I was brought up to the front; but I did not like the job as I expected he was intending to lecture us on our noisy behaviour. But I was soon undeceived, for after a few common questions in a very kind manner, with many 'pauvres hommes' from the ladies, they invited us to come to the house and pointed out the road to it while they proceeded towards it by the garden path. I forgot to mention that, on starting, the little dragoon, who we met at Merrytopol, was taken very ill and we had made him a kind of bed in one of the waggons with our sheepskin coats and overcoats. At the time we arrived opposite the nobleman's' house we were a long distance in front of the waggons, as usual, but had the greater part of the guard with us.

When we arrived at the house we found a whole host of servants of both sexes ready to receive us, and, in all our ragged and lousy condition, we were ushered with great ceremony into the drawing room, and a very nice, well-furnished room, with a good fire, it was. The old gent and the young ladies received us and were very busy in getting us seated. The French came in now, but, contrary to the usual custom, they were only secondary in the estimation of our host, for both him and the young ladies appeared most interested in us, and I was quite the lion of the hour, for I had to explain the dress and markings of our party and when and where they were taken, whether they were wounded or sick, and how they had been treated. Several servants meanwhile were busy in preparing a large table which they loaded with different kinds of viands and decanters and glasses. As soon as the inspection was over our host invited us to begin operations and we very soon obeyed the call. The viands consisted of mutton and roast turkey and goose and fine black pudding, cut in slices, beautiful French rolls and nice butter and a peculiar kind of cheese made by the Russians, plenty of nice grapes and apples and pears and preserved melons. The decanters all contained Walki, but far superior to any we had yet drunk. There was not room at the table for the whole of us so we sat in our original positions and came and helped ourselves at the table and then returned to our places to eat.

Myself and Sgt. Surridge went round the room, one carrying a tray of glasses and the other a decanter in each hand and supplied all hands in turn. Again and again the table was replenished and the several decanters likewise, and the old gent and young ladies appeared greatly pleased at the justice we done their hospitality, and moved about among us inviting us to renew the attack over and over.

After we had eaten as much as we possibly could we were supplied with paper cigarettes and were soon beginning to get merry, for the walki was good and an unlimited supply. The old gent was greatly taken up by a good-looking fellow of the 8th Hussars of the name of Palfreyman, and asked, through me, if he (Palfreyman) would like to marry one of the young ladies. A question that caused some blushing and confusion to our fair hostesses. (Of course, the old gent was joking but he appeared so very serious that I once thought he was in earnest, but he seemed to enjoy the confusion of the ladies vastly.)

One of our men in the height of his gratitude for his kind-ness (and helped a little by the Walki) took the numbers and grenade from his cap and, through me, presented them to the old gent as a souvenir. The old gent was much pleased with the present and declared to me that he would preserve them and prize them for the sake of the English. So there is a set of the 23rd numbers in a nobleman's family in Russia now.

The ladies now enquired if we had any man sick on the road and, upon my telling them that we had a sick comrade in the waggon, they spoke to one of the servants, and soon after placed a large package of tea and a large package of sugar (lump sugar, they have no other in Russia) in my hands, and two preserved melons for the sick man. (And here let me remark that tea in Russia is a very great luxury and only indulged in by the higher classes.)

On departing they enquired if we had any meat and if we would like some. Of course, I said it would be most acceptable. On going outside we found that the guard had been regaled with black bread, preserved melons and cucumbers and walki, and the convicts also. We found that our bountiful host had given us two whole, ready-dressed sheep for the road and they were already in the waggon. The old gentleman and the ladies came to the door to see us off and, when we started we gave three good cheers and the ladies waved their kerchiefs to us and the old nobleman uncovered his grey locks as we cheered. I forget this good old gentleman's name, although he strove to impress it on our memory, but his kindness I will never forget.

We proceeded on our journey in high glee at our good fortune and as usual we pushed on in groups in front of the convoy. After some distance we came to another road diverging slightly to the left of the one we were travelling. Some three or four of the party took this road in mistake and lost their way, but the greater part pursued the right track and reached our destination for the day about 4 o'clock. I must here mention that the weather had begun to get very cold, especially in the night and we had what in England would be called severe frosts. On arrival of the waggons we were billeted as usual on the peasants and, as no one would take charge of the sick man, but rather seemed to shun him, I took the office upon myself. The nobleman's Walki had done its work and most of us were pretty groggy and the greater part began to keep up the spree by sending for more and getting thoroughly drunk, in which laudable pastime they were most willingly assisted by the guard. I kept sober myself to attend to the invalid, and here let me mention his name, for I shall often speak of him. His name, then, was Robert Farquharson, trumpeter in the 4th Light Dragoons and taken in the charge of the Light Cavalry at Balaclava. He was a little fellow, and a Scotsman.

The 4th Light Dragoons (Queen's Own) were commanded at Balaclava by Lord George Paget, a younger son of the Marquis of Anglesey, who had commanded the cavalry at Waterloo. In the charge of the Light

Cavalry Brigade, the 4th Light Dragoons were in the third line, with the 8th Hussars.

Among the fifteen men of the Brigade who were taken prisoner was Trumpeter Farquharson, who described his capture:

". . . shortly I got clear of the crossfire from the batteries and came up to a party of men belonging to different regiments of our Brigade, stragglers, like myself. We kept together and went on until, by and by, we saw the banneroles of a Lancer regiment fluttering above a bank of smoke in which we were enveloped. Thinking it was our own 17th Lancers we made straight for them, only discovering when too late that it was a regiment of Polish Lancers, together with a regiment of Russian Hussars, which had been formed up across the mouth of the valley and were about to advance and sweep away all our men who were still left on the ground. Well, we had no time to consider much about what was to be done, so, keeping well together, we went straight at the enemy and cut our way right through the crowd. We were not yet out of the wood though, for galloping on we immediately found ourselves confronted with a strong force of Cossacks drawn up in line to the rear of the others. We had just to do the same thing by them, and did it, getting through both barriers, to the best of my recollection and belief, without the loss of a man. Pushing onwards, we now saw, about a mile off, the Scots Greys—I think it was them— coming to the cover of our retreat from the field. It was a welcome enough sight, but it wasn't to do me any good. A cannon shot put a sudden stop to my gallop. I saw the horrid thing bounding along the ground, but, for the life of me, I couldn't get out of its way, and it flew up and caught my steed on the head, killing it, of course, there and then. I fell to the ground along with it and in two or three minutes I was surrounded by Cossacks and taken prisoner."

R. S. Farquharson later wrote his adventures in the Crimea and captivity for the Glasgow *Evening Times*, which was published in book form in 1883 in 105 pages as *Reminiscences of Crimean Campaigning and Russian Imprisonment, by one of the Six Hundred.* He tells how he chums up with Sgt. George Newman of the 23rd and tells many of the tales which Newman relates.

I had a pretty busy night with him, but was glad to find him better in the morning. The snow had fallen during the night and lay on the ground 3 inches deep, and winter had evidently set in. We got ready to resume our march at 8 o'clock but found that there were two English and one French missing. They had taken the wrong road the day previous and had not rejoined the party. The sergeant of the escort refused to go on without them and sent out parties in search of them, and the rest of us retired to our billets not the least worried, for a day's rest.

The men soon began to go on the spree again and kept it up the whole day. The two Englishmen came in during the day, but no tidings of the Frenchman (or I should rather call him the Italian, for it was the little Italian corporal). Towards evening I was busy cooking when I heard a wrangle between Sgt. Surridge (my comrade) and a good-looking young soldier of the 41st Regiment, named McDonell. McDonell had taken one of the soldier's firelocks and got some ammunition from one of the pouches and loaded the piece, declaring he would have a shot at something. Surridge, partly by force and partly by persuasion, got the firelock from him and put it away, as it was loaded. I went on with my job and Surridge was doing something else when we heard the report of firearms and soon found that McDonell had possessed himself of the piece and shot the pig belonging to the house where we were stopping. We tracked the pig by the blood on the snow into an old outhouse and found that the ball had gone in at the ham and come out at the shoulder. I was certain it would die and did not know what to do. McDonell was drunk and thought it a bit of fine fun. We pacified the old peasant and his wife for the night by promising to pay for it in the morning, but we well knew we could not perform our promise, for we had but a few copecks among us.

The next morning the pig was found dead enough where we had left him and the old peasant demanded ten roubles for him. We were thunderstruck at the price, for the pig did not weigh over 12 stone, but doubtless the peasant thought of making a good thing of Mr. McDonell's shooting abilities; but when he found we could not pay him even one rouble he got in a rage and ran for the sergeant, who, when he came, told us if we could not pay and settle the matter he must make McDonell a close prisoner, and ironed, until he came to the next town where he would be severely punished.

McDonell was now sorry for his fool-hardiness and tried to beg off, but without effect. We offered the old peasant what money we had, but he would not accept and went and fetched a kind of notary who made out a written report of the circumstance and gave it to the sergeant to give to the authorities upon his arrival. This made the case look even more serious, and the sgt. commenced to put irons on McDonell, when in came Jack-of-Clubs. He asked the reason for the scene before him and when I told him he quickly changed the aspect of the affair. He caught the old notary by the back of the neck and soon kicked him out of the house. He then collared the Russian sgt. and knocked his head against the wall until he shouted again, and all the time he kept abusing the English for allowing the sgt. to iron one or our party. The old sgt. turned nearly black in the face with the pressure of Jack's fingers and gasped out that he would take the irons off again. Upon which Jack released him, but stood by him while he took off the offensive irons, jabbering and gesticulating like a monkey.

As soon as McDonell was released Jack shouldered the carcass of the pig and threw the old peasant a rouble and stalked out of the house in triumph, followed by the whole of us. We fully expected a glorious row when the sergeant reached the rest of his people, but he only cursed a little and soon laughed at the whole concern. Jack-of-Clubs, when he reached his billet, got a knife and opened the pig and declared that the pork was as good as any in France. He cleaned it and washed it and then brought it to me saying that we could have it, but must repay him the rouble he had given to the old peasant for it when next we got paid, and in the meantime we could sell the pork among our own party on credit and he himself would buy some of it. To this we all agreed and the Italian corporal having returned we set forward once more on our journey.

The Italian corporal had had good times of it during his absence, for he had been kindly taken into a gentleman's house and lodged and fed during the whole time and now returned with a good stock of shirts, stockings, trowsers &c.

That night, on reaching our billet, we roasted the bristles off the pig and cut him up in joints and made Jack a present of a leg and loin. Some of the remainder we sold at one copeck per pound and the rest we ate in our own mess. We had pork galore as long as it lasted, I assure you, and I cannot recollect anything of any importance happening until we reached Ekaterinaslav, the next large town on our route.

The former Ekaterinaslav was founded, as the name implies, by Catherine the Great in 1784. The main

street, described by Newman, is the Catherine Prospecki—
nearly three miles long. The town is now called Dnepro-
petrosk.

Our money was again due on the day we entered this town,
in consequence of our having stayed in the village with the
pig. This town is a very large one and we marched down the
main street amid a crowd of eager spectators. It was a very
long street with many fine houses on each side, and a gravel
walk on each side, with two lines of trees. There were a great
many well-dressed people walking about and some tolerable
equipages with fashionably dressed females driving up and
down the road (for, like all other towns in Russia they have
but a very short distance of good roading and on this the
gentlefolks would take their airings).

We were taken to some kind of an office, where the roll was
called and questions asked as to who wanted shirts or boots
or gloves or caps (a piece of humbug that made us believe we
were going to get a better fit-out). After waiting here some
time we were marched back through the main street to another
house. We stopped here some hours and fully expected we
were to be paid here, but no such thing.

During the time we stopped here we had several visitors,
some of whom brought us some apples and some cigarettes
and one, a French roll each. At last, just as night was
falling, we were marched off again and in about half an hour
arrived at a large house which, from the grated windows and
sentries round it, proclaimed it to be some sort of gaol; but the
governor (for such we took him to be) declared he had no
room for us, and we were marched off to another about
500 yards from the other and directly opposite to it. It was too
dark to see what kind of place it was, but we passed under a
large arched gateway with large, heavy-barred gates reaching
to the top of the arch at each end. Between them was a guard

house and two sentries. After waiting some time we were admitted and conducted up a large flight of stone steps first and wooden steps after, to an upper floor where there were two rooms, with a sentry inside to take care of us. The French took possession of the outer room, for each room ran into the other, but, as the rooms were small and would not hold us comfortably separate, we included seven or eight of our men with the French. As soon as we got in we discovered pencil writing on the walls in places, which we found were the work of the Dragoons taken at Balaclava and preceded us on the road and had occupied these rooms.

The writing told us to beware of sharpers, especially a clergyman who styled himself an Armenian missionary and was a prisoner in the prison. Then there was a caution not to let the governor mess us, but demand our money and liberty to buy and cook what was thought proper. There was several other remarks and the names and regiments of the Dragoons, but too tedious to mention. The Governor soon came to visit us and offered to subsist us, but we would not agree to it and demanded our pay for that day and liberty to go and buy eatables, for we were hungry. But he told us that we should get no money while there and that we should stop there four days more; offered to supply us with provisions once more, but we stoutly stuck up for the money and he left us in a tiff. We got no provisions of any kind that night, but went to bed supperless and snoozed until morning. The room was warm and comfortable (barring the lice and fleas), being heated by two ovens.

The next morning we waited impatiently for our pay, for hunger began to be oppressive. We waited several hours in vain, but about 11 o'clock an officer came round, to whom we made a complaint about our money; and about two hours after a clerk and an officer and the Governor came and paid us at the rate of 20 copecks per day, and liberty was given for eight of us to go to market once a day for the whole. The party was soon made up, but I did not go. After the party returned and we had satisfied our hunger on bread and butter, honey and fried fish we enquired for some person to wash for us, for we were determined to treat ourselves to a clean shirt (and we wanted it badly for I had not had a clean shirt to put on since the day before our army left Varna, which was the beginning of September, and now it was nearly Christmas. In fact I believe it was about the 15th December). To manage to get a clean one we were obliged to pull off the old dirty ones and go without, while they were being washed and dried. We found a woman prisoner who offered to do as we wanted for 20 copeks each, to which we agreed, and she took our old shirts away, promising we should have them next day, but she kept us without them for three days.

In the evening, to amuse ourselves, we started all manner of games and I was nearly choked in "cock fighting". This game is played by tying the hands below the knees, while sitting on the ground, and then passing a stout stick between your elbows and knees, which trussed a man up like a ball. Two of such are placed opposite each other and try to overbalance each other by lifting up each other's toes with their own. When upset they roll about in a truly laughable fashion. I had a short time before eaten a goodly quantity of 'stir-about' and, when I entered the circle against one of the 7th Regt., I was pretty tight. We manoeuvered for a time and then I had the fortune to toss him and he rolled twice over. He cut such a ridiculous figure I had a complete fit of laughter at him. His second soon put him to rights again and while I was in the midst of my laughter he gave me a trip up and I rolled over like a porpoise and the 'stir-about' ran up in my throat and between that and the laughing I was near pegging out, nor could the others help me. At last they saw my danger and released me and by vigorous thumping on the back eventually put me to rights, but I don't remember ever being so near kicking the bucket.

The following morning I was one of the market party and cut a dash with my old coatee buttoned up close to hide that I had not a shirt on. The market place was tremendous dirty, the sludge was nearly knee deep, but we had got used to dirt and filth, as we had to many other unpleasant things, and stumped through it merrily. I was particularly struck by one thing, and that was that nearly every house had a large tub on a platform on the roof, and I thought there must be a great many coopers in the town. But I soon found that those tubs were supposed to be kept full of water in case of fire.

As we were coming back we met several of the sailors who had arrived the evening before. There was a great deal of news to be exchanged on both sides and among other things they told us of a battle they had had with the Turks that were taken with them. It appeared that, on reaching the prison (the one where we were refused) the night before, they were all, Turks and English, put together in one large stone-floored room. The sailors never liked the Turks because of their dirty filthy habits, and the sailors drew a chalk line across the floor and intimated to the Turks that they were to keep on one side of it and the English on the other, an arrangement that did not meet with the entire approbation of the Bonno Johnnys who continued to trespass on the English territory. At last one of them came over and began to louse himself among the English, not killing the lice but depositing them carefully on the floor. Skin and blood couldn't stand this and the boatswain, a raw-boned, very strong man from Nova Scotia, genteely kicked the offending Turk to his own side of the room. Upon which the Turks, headed by their three officers, made a grand attack upon the whole of the sailors. The room was long and narrow and the boatswain and several others formed line across it, and, being well versed in the art of self defence, knocked down the Turks as fast as they came up. As they could not all come to close quarters at the same time, those in the rear started throwing whatever came to hand, and boots, slippers, bundles and pieces of bread were sent against each other in quick order. But one of the sailors, coming through the town, had bought a large quantity of apples for his own mastication and those were produced and used as missiles against the enemy and very soon forced them to retire, followed by the victorious English until they had drove them out of the room. The Governor now came in and, as he could not reconcile the parties, he put the Turks in another room. The sailors were greatly elated by their victory and termed it 'The battle of boots and apples'.

This afternoon we had some French gentlemen come to visit us and they invited the whole of the French to dinner the next day. An invitation that was not offered twice without being accepted at once, I assure you.

We passed the evening as the ones before and the night, as usual in prisons, lying on the boards. We never fancied the prisons for this reason in particular, as we could generally get some straw to lie on when in a peasant's hut.

The next morning there was a great rubbing and scrubbing among the French to get ready for their dinner party. They started about 2 o'clock and returned about 6 o'clock in a merry state, and bringing several bottles of wine with them. They gave a great description of the kindness they had received and showed us some new shirts and stockings they had had given them, besides one rouble each, as they were coming away, which Jack-of-Clubs collected as usual and put in the general purse (his old leg of stocking) which he carried himself.

This evening we had no games as usual as some of the party had brought two packs of cards, which proved a stronger source of amusement than cock fighting.

The next morning we were visited by the French gentlemen,

who brought us a good supply of Turkish tobacco, considered the best in the country. I longed to ask one of them to give me a shirt but was ashamed to do so. When they were gone, myself and several others cut pieces off our old greatcoats to mend our old trousers with and as we had not a second pair to put on we sat in a state of nudity on the floor, cutting, sewing and contriving; but we first took the precaution of placing a sentry on the door to give the alarm in case of a surprise by any visitors, for we did not like the idea of our modesty being shocked by the abrupt entrance of any females. We also cut pieces of cloth and fastened them inside our caps to cover our ears, with strings to tie under the chin.

I have forgotten to say anything about the minister, but will now. We had several visits from him during the first two days. He spoke broken English and told us he was a missionary employed by a society in England; that he was an Armenian by birth and that he had been preaching and teaching far up in the country in a very cold place; that he had been confined for his preaching and had travelled a long, very long, distance down the country towards Odessa where he expected to have been set at liberty and sent to England; but then war breaking out had made the authorities determine to keep him here. He had been a prisoner about 20 months. He did tell us his name but it was such an outlandish name that I forgot it. He was a grey-haired old man, rather short and stout. He received 25 copecks per day for his subsistence and had a separate apartment allotted to him away from the common prisoners. He invited us to his room for prayers, but as he could only preach in the Slavonian tongue we did not go. We gained considerable information from him, especially Russian words and sentences, which we wrote down.

The next day Jack-of-Clubs, while picking a couple of geese, laid his purse (or, rather, stocking leg) by his side. He turned from the spot a few minutes, when somebody emptied his stocking of its contents but generously left the stocking to be refilled. Jack actually gave us a dance in his rage but he did not know who to blame as there were several Russian soldiers in the room at the time as they were relieving guard. He stormed and swore for a long time but eventually sat down in despair, and a pretty picture of misery he cut, I assure you.

We sent for the woman who took our shirts to bring them back, but could not get them. On the next morning we were given the word to prepare to march and just as we were about to start the woman brought our shirts. We had no cause to complain of her want of energy in washing, for most of them were in large sized ribbons, and would puzzle a Philadelphia lawyer to find the road into some of them, they had so many false entrances.

We started about 10 o'clock and when we got outside the prison we observed what appeared to be a whole regt. drawn up in line with the front rank faced about. Each man had a long stick, as thick as my thumb, in his hand. Some poor devil was about to run the gauntlet for I had often heard of it. We all wanted to stop to view the punishment, but a mounted officer rode up and compelled us to move on.

We were taken to the same office where they had so kindly enquired about our boots, gloves, shirts etc. We stayed here for a long time, but at last got paid our money for the ensuing march and two days due while in prison, but they could not pay us the day we came into the town.

There was a young lady came here to see us, who spoke English fluently. She said that she was the daughter of a French father and an English mother, born in France but brought up and educated at Richmond in Surrey. She was much shocked at our destitute appearance and pitied us much. She sent for her husband (a Frenchman) and when he came sent him off again somewhere. We crowded round her in a complete mob, drinking in all she told us of the country and people, for she had a sweet voice that fascinated the whole of us. She took down the address of the married men's wives and promised to write to them about their husbands. She went into the office and argued the point for us about the day's pay we were short of and got it for us. Her husband returned with a servant loaded with shirts and long, thick stockings (but not many of the first) and good woollen gloves. She commenced giving them out herself but the men pressed in upon her so much in their eagerness to obtain all they could that she gave them to me. I served them all out to our people as I considered the French were well off. There were but a few shirts and those I distributed to most of those who had none but could not complete them all, but there was stockings and gloves enough to supply each with one pair, and one pair of gloves over, which I kept myself.

She said she was very sorry she was not rich enough, for she would like to supply us all with everything we required, but what money she had she would give us. With that she sent for change for a note and gave us each a 20 copeck silver piece. We thanked her very much for her kindness and she remained with us all the time—some hours—we stopped there, although it was a very cold day.

We were surprised by the arrival of the sailors and Turks, but soon found that they were to march with us. The Turks were supplied with boots but none of the rest of us.

About four o'clock in the afternoon we bade farewell to our kindhearted visitor and commenced the march again. The day was bitter cold and I found my ear-lugs very comfortable. When we left the town we had to cross the river Dnieper again and it was very wide and rapid stream here. Before we got to the embarking place several of us went into a Walki shop to get a glass to keep out the cold.

We had a new guard with us leaving the town and they wanted us to march like felons when first we started, but we would not do it and the cranky old sergeant was wild to find his authority set at nought. When he saw us go into the Walki shop he collected some of his men and tried to turn us out, and a row ensued. I got my glass and was walking away from the house quickly towards the boat when somebody gave me a thrust in the back. I turned and found it was the sergeant, so I made motions to him not to do it again and gave him to understand that I would give him a taste of my stick if he did, but he spat at me and tried to strike my face; but I warded it off and gave him a rap with my stick that made his head ring. Upon which he outs with his cutlass and we had a bit of sword practice, he with the cutlass and I with the stick, and I fancy I gave him some raps he did not relish; but Jack-of-Clubs came up and took him dirty with a topper on the head that laid him at full stretch on the ground.

We then walked easily down to the boats, and the sergeant was carried in by three or four of his guard and laid on the bottom of the boat, where he soon got alright again and was civil enough to us afterwards.

By the time we had crossed the river it was dusk and bitter cold, and we had 17 versts to go. Our march after we had crossed the river lay for a long distance along the sands by the river side, and bitter cold we found the wind off the water. Our guard, by some means, missed the road and kept us waiting an hour and a half while they found it, for it was now very dark. At length they found it, and I could find it was a new Macadamised road with a hand rail on both sides. Every here and there they had placed large stones to keep the vehicles to the centre of the road. Those stones proved a great annoyance to us in the dark, for we kept stumbling over them and injuring our shins and every few yards there was deep drains cut in the pathway to carry off the water from the road into which we kept stumbling. So that, what with cold, the stones, and the drains, our march was anything but comfortable, and to make it all serene we had no less than three waggons break down at different times, to the eminent danger of losing what traps we were possessed of.

Seymour wrote:

"The roads of Southern Russia are mere tracks, and those on which Post communications are established have, earth thrown up at their sides and at intervals, conical mounds of earth or stones to indicate the way."

These would have contrasted sharply with the fine, dry gravelled Turnpikes of England, the finest in the world, which had been pioneered by Macadam and Telford, to which Newman refers.

At last we reached the village where we were to rest for the night. It was about eleven o'clock and we had to knock the peasants up to get a lodging.

The next morning we assembled at eight o'clock, in the village, to resume our march, and Jack-of-Clubs came to me and told me he had lost a bottle of butter from his provisions bag and also that he had seen a man of my regiment with his hand in the bag and he believed he was the thief. I called the man up and told him of it, but he firmly denied all knowledge of the affair; but Jack persisted in his statement and further said that he believed it was he who stole the money from his purse. This was nigh causing a fight but we managed to part them and proceeded on our route.

This evening the cold had increased and we were billeted as usual in a peasant's hut. We found great difference in our style of living through the increase in our pay, for we could buy a goose and potatoes for supper, and this is the way we did it. There was nine of us messing together who always made it a point to lodge in the same house. When we arrived at our lodging two or three would start off to buy something for supper. If we had a goose we always picked the largest we could find and they would cost between 20 to 30 copecks each. So we used to get goose for a sum ranging from 6d to 1s, which could not be bought in London for less than 7 or 8 shillings. Sometimes we would buy a sucking pig and sometimes pork or mutton, but our cooking was always the same: namely, we would buy a lot of murphies from the people of the house (for the Russian peasants keep all their own provisions) which, after washing, we would put in a pot and then into the oven to boil. Then we would cut the goose, or whatever it might be, into small pieces and put it in another pot with plenty of water, onions, salt, pepper and any vegetables we could get hold of to make soup. Thus, we used to have soup of pork, goose or sucking pig often. The whole was then put in the oven to boil and when the murphies were done they were pulled out and all hands but the cook's would set about knocking their jackets off. They were then put in the pot again and placed in the mouth of the oven, without water, to dry. As soon as the goose or meat was done the fat was carefully skimmed off and put over the potatoes. The soup was always served up first (for we like to be fashionable) and as there is always a good supply of wooden spoons in every Russian domicile, we used to make a combined attack.

There was also a great deal of economy in having soup first, for we were always very hungry after our day's march and would lay into the well-breaded soup without mercy, and so not have any too much room for the solids that came after. By this plan we always found a good sized goose or sucking pig sufficient. In the morning we generally managed to buy two or three jugs of milk and we would have a milk and bread breakfast, either hot or cold according to circumstance.

The cold had increased greatly and the snow was falling and drifting. We had a good supper of goose soup etc., when in came a very tidily dressed man for a peasant. He saluted the people of the house who seemed to know him, and gave us to understand that he was a Pole and that he had been a soldier under Napoleon and had served in several campaigns. He sent for some Walki and we sat and chatted for a long time and smoked our pipes, but got tired at last and wanted to lie down and asked for some straw to spread on the floor for a bed, and we all laid down, but one man of the regiment of the name of Argue. I asked him why did he not lie down as we did and he replied he did not like stripping before the Pole as he had got no shirt. But the Pole showed no signs of going away, but got into a confab with the old man of the house.

At last Argue, in despair of his going, began to strip and shewed his bare buff. The Pole began to strip also and we wondered what he intended when, to our amazement, he pulled off his shirt and presented it to Argue saying that he had another one at home and he had only 7 versts to go. Thus, he had got seven versts walk in this cold night without a shirt, through his kindness. I mention this last fact particularly because I thought and think now it was the kindest action I ever saw from one stranger to another.

The next day on the march we were talking of this among the sailors, who were surprised to hear we were so bad off for shirts and promised to give us some. We had a long march this day and it was late before we got in and many of the convicts were completely knocked up, so that we had a halt day the next day to refresh them a little. Early the next morning the sailors came to our house and gave Sgt. Surridge a lot of shirts and drawers and several pairs of trowsers, which Surridge distributed as well as he could. I got a blue check shirt and I was very thankful for it as I could now and then have a clean one. After the distribution we made a collection and sent for some Walki, and the boatswain, who was a good fifer, sent for his fife and we had dancing galore and a merry day.

The next day on the march, some of the Turks, too lazy

to walk, got up on the waggon, and some of them sat upon the sailors' bread, which did not improve its appearance, you may be sure, and the sailors declared it actually tasted bad after the operation of squeezing. However, in the afternoon a sailor caught one of them making a seat of his tammy bag and told the fellow to move off, but the fellow either did not or would not understand and the sailor knocked him off the waggon. Several Turks ran up to take the part of their comrade, which caused a general row, for the English, both soldiers and sailors, ran up to assist their countryman and, as we all carried good sticks there was soon a glorious shindy; but although the Bonno Johnny's were treble our numbers they got a precious whipping. The boatswain performed prodigies of valour, for among other things he was a good single stick player and he measured them for tin hats as fast as they came near him and, when the battle was over, they had many who were obliged to ride for they could not walk. The finish of the battle was that the Turks were compelled to march in the rear and having some waggons told off for their especial accommodation and they were on no account to interfere with ours.

We soldiers despised the whole of the Turkish race for their cowardice in running away from the batteries at Balaclava and letting the Russians right in upon our lines and thereby bringing on the battle of Balaclava when so many of our light cavalry were killed and taken. The sailors detested them for their filthy habits and for making their ship lousy, while we soldiers could not forget the hardships we had undergone in their country. So I must own the Turks were never regarded with any favour for any of us.

The Turks had been responsible for the defence of five redoubts which had been constructed to guard the main east–west road, just north of Balaclava town. Early on the 25th October the Russians had sent heavy detachments of troops and artillery against these redoubts, as a preliminary to an attack on the British supply base at Balaclava itself. When it was clear that no support was coming, the Turks, outnumbered twelve to one, withdrew, leaving half their number, dead.

Colonel Lysons wrote in some disgust: "All the Turks ran away, left their redoubts and hid in holes in Balaclava". How justified was his disgust is a matter often discussed, but it was the misunderstanding of the order to recapture these redoubts and their guns which lead to the disasterous Charge of the Light Brigade.

That night some of them met some of our men returning from looking after victuals and belaboured them unmercifully, so the next morning there was another general row and the Turks again got the worst of it. During the whole of this time the dysentery had not left me, although I was nothing near so bad as I had been. But I also began to suffer again with the toothache and that, combined with the other, made me anything but comfortable.

There was nothing else occurred until we reached a dirty, miserable, tumbledown town called Nova Moscow.

This is the town of Novomoskovsk, 350 miles from Sebastopol. They had now been travelling for about seven weeks.

CHAPTER FIVE

Hospital
25th December – 19th January

FRENCH INFANTRY OF THE LINE
From *The Illustrated London News*
2nd December 1854

We arrived at Nova Moscow on Christmas Eve and all hands determined to be jolly. We were kept in the market place of the town a long time as we believed for the purpose of finding billets for us, but, after waiting a long time, they marched us off to a prison; but Jack-of-Clubs while waiting had not been idle, for he had made the acquaintance of some old lady who had given him two roubles and four beautiful large live geese, which he carried across his shoulder and they gave us plenty of much sweeter music than the convicts' irons.

When we arrived at the prison we found it a low building surrounded by a high picketing or stockade and a large pair of gates under an archway, with a guard under the archway. Jack-of-Clubs did not like the appearance of the place and soon persuaded all hands not to go in, and, upon the guard telling us to enter, we all refused, and Jack was in his glory at once. We demanded billets and would not go in. The old sergeant of the guard and the sergeant of the prison guard were thunder-struck at our contumacy, and for a time did not know what to do. But at last they sent off a messenger for an officer who, when he came, tried to persuade us to go in, but without success. He then invited Jack-of-Clubs to enter to view the place, which he did; but when he returned he gave it an awful character. In consequence of which we were more determined than ever not to go in.

The officer, seeing how things were going, got the whole of the guards together and surrounded us and then charged us at the point of the bayonet. When Jack-of-Clubs got in he took possession of a small room adjoining the women's apartments and commenced to make himself comfortable, when he was interrupted by the Turkish officers who had been sent to the room by the officer. They requested Jack to depart, but he refused to do so and one of them took hold of Jack to turn him out, when he hit him a blow that made his mouth about half an inch wider. This was near causing another row, but the Russian officer came in and settled the matter by sending the three officers out into billets.

Jack then came to me and said that the room was large enough to hold my party, if we liked to come, which of course we did. There was now a row that the guard would not let any of us out to market, and we collected around the gate in a mob shouting to be let out. There was a wicket gate in one of the large ones but the sentry would not open it; but Jack-of-Clubs settled the job by offering him a 20 copeck piece to let him out— a bribe very hard to resist by a Russian sentry. He drew back the bolt very slowly and quietly, but as soon as the door began to shew signs of being loosened there was a general rush towards it. The old sentry tried with all his might to close it again but in vain, for he was forced by the pressure up against the wall between that and the door, and there he stuck as straight as an arrow nearly pressed to death, while the whole party of us who wanted to go out scampered off towards the town, followed by the guard; but we outran them and at last they turned back.

On going out I had been entrusted with two roubles from one and another, besides the money of a collection, for Walki. I went first to the Walki shop and paid for the Walki and left it there until I came back, for I had to buy a supply of provisions. I had brought some bread and some fried fish (the only cooked thing I could find) and then went to another stall for more, when I found to my dismay that I had lost my bag and money. I searched about in vain and was obliged to give it up for a bad job. I returned with what things I had bought, and told of my loss. It caused much disappointment but little grumbling as I promised to pay it back as soon as I could. Jack-of-Clubs also brought in a good stock of Walki and we clubbed the two lots together and had a very merry Christmas Eve in spite of my loss.

While we were carousing, the officer who had turned us in came in and two others with him, one of whom spoke French fluently. Jack-of-Clubs was giving us some kind of war dance, with a large bottle in one hand and a tin cup in the other, as they entered. The one who spoke French commenced telling Jack that spirits were not allowed in the prison, and the other, who had been present at the row with Jack and the Turkish officers, began and told the other, who appeared the head of the whole, all about it. But Jack took off his cap and made a great speech about it, which, although I could not understand one third of it, I was sure was very flattering to them, for instead of kicking up a rumpus they drank with us and then sent for more.

The remainder of the party were enjoying themselves also very merrily, and we could hear the boatswain's fife going ahead and the dancers making the old prison shake again. I dare say the old building never had such a merry party in it before or since.

The next day was Christmas Day and there was only one Walki shop on all our road that day, but we pulled up for it at night and astonished the Russian peasants with our singing and dancing. The next day our heads were rather queer, but we done a long day's march notwithstanding, and went to our litter of straw sober alright.

The next morning one of the men came to me with a proposition to pay off my debts, which was that he should get up a raffle for something and they would all join in and the money thus collected would pay off my loss and put me square once more. The great obstacle of which was that I had nothing to offer for the raffle except a new pair of stockings given me by the lady at Ekaterinaslav, and I did not like parting with them; but I was overruled, and that evening arrived in a town whose name I forget and were placed in a prison again. Here my stockings were put up to the raffle and were won by one of the sailors. The price was three copeks per member and the proceeds cleared me from debt and about 20 copeks in hand. I was all right once more now and out of debt.

My comrade Surridge was taken ill during the night and another man, a corporal of my own regiment, went to hospital in the morning.

About 8 o'clock a clerk came and paid us for the next march and we were then marched out of the prison into the market place opposite, where we were halted and allowed to go and buy what we wanted. We were here joined by a French Artillery man who had been taken in a sortie and had been in hospital in the town. He was very thin and emaciated and appeared very weak.

As we stood in the market place I noticed a very decent looking man with a black thorn stick in his hand, and I tried to get him to change with me, but he did not seem to understand me; but one of our party, McDonell, who shot the poor pig, teased him until he got it. We now left the town and proceeded on our road as usual, pushing far in front of the waggons and convicts. We met a whole regiment of recruits coming down the country, who seemed to think that we had made our escape; for, after we passed them some distance, they gave chase and overtook us and wanted to force us to go back, a proceeding that would have certainly ended in another row only for the timely arrival of some of our escort, who made all serene.

That night there was a heavy fall of snow and the next morning Jack-of-Clubs again tried to get a motion that we should not march that day, but he only partly succeeded this time and we started about 10 o'clock. This day, on the road, one of the French stole a kind of scarf from a Walki shop, and the woman who owned it followed us to our halting place and found it on him. Jack-of-Clubs was very indignant that one of the French party should so disgrace themselves, and he took off his coat and gave him a hiding.

This night I had the toothache very bad. So much so that I could not eat my supper. It continued the whole night, and the next morning the old woman of the house made signs to me that a man in the village could cure it. I was happy to hear this and the fellow was sent for with all speed, and I made sure of having my troublesome tooth out. The man came after a little time and I noticed the little old lady of the house began crossing herself as soon as this man entered the room. You must know that in every Russian dwelling there is always a picture of the Virgin Mary, or some other saint, in a corner of the dwelling room, and it is the same in all dwellings from the highest to the lowest, and they pay their devotions to the picture, bowing and crossing themselves at the same time. I showed the old chap my tooth and he shook his head in a very wise manner, but struck the bargain that I should give him 3 copecks when he had finished, which I readily promised to do. He then set to work to pray and sing and bow and cross to the old picture, the old woman of the house keeping chorus with him. He kept on about 20 minutes, me wondering all the time how long he would be praying before he began drawing. At length he turned suddenly round and caught me by the jaws and forced my mouth open and blowed in it three times (and worse, the old fellow had been eating garlic). He then told me to spit three times on the floor, which I did, and he held out his hand for payment, assuring me I was cured. I could not help laughing at the old man, and all the rest of the party joined in, to the evident vexation of the old man and woman, who made signs to us that we should certainly go below to the warm regions some day, and doubtless they thought us terrible heretics. But I paid the old man and gave the old lady 2 copecks for coming coal-box.

I got one of my party to tie a piece of wadding round the tooth to keep the cold air from it and then we turned out to be ready for the march, and a fine joking I got about the tooth-curer.

When we got to the place of starting we found several peasants on horseback armed with tremendous cudgills, who had been called upon to assist our escort in getting us off, through the motion by Jack-of-Clubs the day before that we should not march, only when we liked. When we started this morning the sergeant still kept those fellows, and sent one of them out to shut the Walki shops before we came up to them: a proceeding we found very displeasing to our whole party.

The bullying of the mounted peasants did not suit our party at all and many polite names were passed among and between the soldiers, peasants and our men. Jack-of-Clubs, who had picked up a deal of Russian, let fly among them, and the artillery man, who also learnt a good deal while in hospital, bandied civilities and courteous expressions with one of the soldiers until the soldier got his steam up and knocked the artillery man down with the butt of his firelock. As soon as he had done so, Jack-of-Clubs measured the soldier for a tin hat and sent him sprawling. Another soldier ran at Jack with his levelled bayonet and would have certainly given Jack his quietus, but McDonell of the 41st was standing by with the stick in his hand he got from the person I mentioned in the last town. He struck the soldier a tremendous blow on the bridge of the nose, and I believe killed him on the spot.

There was now a general fight, some of the men closed with the soldiers and took their firelocks from them, and bloody noses and black eyes and broken heads were plentifully served out among the combatants. The peasants rode up to take part, but most of them were soon unhorsed and they found to their sorrow that they had armed themselves very badly, for their cudgills were so heavy that they could not wield them fast enough for either attack or defence. Seeing this, many of them turned to the right about and beat a hasty retreat, hastened by some of our men, who had got hold of some firelocks, pretending to load. The fight did not last long but was pretty sharp while it lasted, and after it was over they soon made friends again as far as appearances went. The firelocks were returned on condition the embargo should be taken off the dram shops, and no more peasants called upon.

We then proceeded on the road, which was enlivened every now and then by the old sergeant making signs of their being hanged.

And now comes my turn. My tooth began to ache dreadfully, so much so that I could not keep up and instead of being in front as usual, I lagged behind; my little comrade, trumpeter Farquharson also keeping me company. The first Walki shop we came to we went into and tried to get a glass, so that, by holding the spirit in my mouth I might ease the pain; but there was a soldier there who would not allow me to have any but, by shewing him what I wanted it for and giving him a glass, prevailed on him to let me have it. We started off together after the convoy, and as I could not get on fast enough we got gradually more and more to the rear, but made it a point to call in each Walki shop we reached for a reviver, and I gradually lost the tooth ache. The soldier and us came along merrily and quickly enough for some distance until we reached another dram shop and, as usual, went inside for another drop.

Me and the soldier had two glasses each here, as usual one of which I drank and the other was ready. I gave a 30 copeks piece for what we had. I happened to turn my back for a minute or two, and when I came back I saw Mr. Soldier coolly pocketing my change. Of course I asked him to give it up, but he refused. Again and again I tried with the same success, and at last he shook his fist in my face, and this time Farquharson joined in, but to no avail. I could stand it no longer and gave him such a crack in the eye that his face swelled instantly down to his mouth. He slapped his hand to his face and ran out of the house, as we thought to overtake the party and tell a yarn against us. But no such thing, for he had been gone but a few minutes when he returned with five or six lumping fellows and they all commenced an attack upon us.

I recognised three of the peasants as belonging to our mounted party in the morning. We got back into the corner as quickly as possible and struck out right and left for dear life, but they closed on us. We had knives, very much like pig-butchers' knives, for which I had made a leathern case and wore in a belt round my waist. Finding myself so closely set, I out with the knife and dealt out right and left, but the soldier struck me on the arm with his piece and rendered me powerless and I became an early capture. They pummelled me as long as I could stand on my legs, and when I fell down one held me down by the hair and another by the feet while the remainder kicked and jumped on me and the soldier thrashed me with the butt of his piece. Two of them took a great fancy to my face, for they bestowed all their kicks on my countenance and jumped on it several times, and by the time they had finished their sport I was not able to move. I noticed one of them turn very pale during this pleasant exercise and put his hand in his shirt and leave the room and I somehow think that I must have touched him with the knife.

Meanwhile my little companion was giving a good account of himself, but he too was soon overpowered. They seemed to think there was no chance of our escaping, for they left us lying across the doorway, while they sat down to some black bread and fried fish and Walki, and they amused themselves by throwing the fish bones and pieces of black bread cracker at us as we lay. A piece of appreciation that galled me more than the whopping.

After they had finished their repast one of them brought a

long rope with which they tied my hands and then drew my legs and feet up towards my back and made them fast to my hands, a very comfortable position, I assure you. They did the same for my companion and then they drove a sleigh to the shop into the back part of which we were unceremoniously tumbled, and the soldier got in and they drove off towards the halting place.

While we had been thus engaged it had been snowing heavily and the tracks on the ground made by our party, who were now a long way ahead, were completely covered.

By and by I heard the tinkle of bells approaching and knew that it must be a sleigh. I managed to pull over to one side and could see that the sleigh had two lights, which proclaimed it to be somebody of consequence, and I determined to make one effort for liberation from my bonds. So, when the strange sleigh drew up, I shouted in French for it to stop. The soldier and driver tried to stop me from calling by putting their hands over my mouth, but the mischief was done and the strange sleigh pulled up and ordered our driver to stop also. He then asked in French who called, and I answered I was an English prisoner of war. He came to the back of the sleigh, but could not make me out for it was now pitch dark; so he called to his sleigh for a light, in Russian, and some person brought him the flambeaux.

I saw he was a good-looking young officer with a cloak on, and I told him as well as I could how I had been treated. He ordered the soldier to take the rope off us, and it was soon done and we sat upright, and he gave us a dram of Walki from his flask and then took the whip from the driver and gave Mr. Soldier a few cuts with it that made him shout 'O, be joyful' to another tune. After which he bade me adieu, telling me I had not more than 3 versts to go to the town, and that he was on express duty and in a hurry, and drove off.

We then drove off as before, with the soldier in a more civil mood and I soon dozed off. I was suddenly awakened from my slumbers by my companion shaking me and pointing to the soldier and driver, who were speaking to each other in great excitement, and the driver took to whipping up the horses and urging them to their topmost speed. I could not understand much of what was said but got the gist of it.

"Wolves, by God, they are after us," I shouted to Farquharson, and looking behind and a long way off, saw a dark mass speedily moving across the wide expanse of snow. The horses evidently knew what was the matter now, as well as we did, but in a few moments we saw the lights ahead and towards this port the horses madly galloped. It was an exceedingly close shave, and we had not reached our destination too early because, when the driver of our machine got out to unharness the horses, a large wolf, which had got into the courtyard before the gates were closed, bounded away.

We were taken into a kind of office where our names were put down and I was the subject of amusement to several clerks, through my ornamented countenance, but the soldier said something to them that caused a big change in their behaviour, for they treated me with the appearance of respect and brought me some water and soap and towels to wash the blood from my face. I fancy the soldier told them I was able to speak to their officers, or they would not have changed their manner as they did.

After I had washed, the soldier beckoned me to come with him to my billet, but we hesitated putting ourselves in his power so completely and at last refused to go altogether with him, for had he thought proper to attack us we could have done nothing in defence. One of the clerks enquired the cause of our hesitation of the soldier, who appeared to have guessed the reason correctly. The clerk then offered to accompany us, which we accepted, and we started off together, but very slowly, for it was with great difficulty I could walk at all. We had gone some distance when I heard some person call me and soon found it was one of my messmates, who had been on the lookout for me. When he came up he did not know me, such a complete change had the two peasants made in my appearance. He took me to the house and got me supper, but I was past eating and could not touch it, but was very glad to get a lie down.

The next morning I got a look at myself in the glass and I certainly cut a pretty figure. I had two pretty black eyes and my nose seemed disposed to cover my whole face. My mouth was swelled a prodigious size and my jaws were so stiff I could not open my mouth to get a bit of bread in, and, to finish it all, my face was a complete scab all over, and my body was covered in bruises, and my arm, where I had been hit with the firelock, was awfully swollen and nearly as large as my thigh.

Luckily one of the men had the bowl of an old teaspoon, with which they managed to put a little bread and milk in my mouth. I wanted to go in hospital but was told there was none before we had finished the day's march. When we were about to resume the march the men made a bed on one of the waggons and covered me up with old coats and sheepskins. I saw the soldier who had got me in this plight, and I must say it gave me great satisfaction to see that his eye was completely closed up and blacked to a nicety. The day was bitter cold and, in spite of the covering heaped on me, I shivered again and by the time we reached our destination I was very ill. Before we started this morning an officer came to us, and all but me fell in, and their sticks taken from them, and gave them to understand that they must not carry sticks to kill soldiers with in future.

The rest of the party reached the town before me and the waggons, and when I arrived I saw Jack-of-Clubs in earnest conversation with several officers and soon learned he was arguing the point concerning the fray, and he succeeded very well in putting the blame on the soldiers, and we heard no more of the circumstance from the Russian.

I tried to get into hospital this evening, but could not be admitted until the morning. Some of the men spread their cloaks on the prison floor (for we were put into the prison for the night) and I was laid on them and covered up, but the shivering would not leave me and I passed a wretched night.

Farquharson had the scurvy very bad in his legs and determined to go into hospital with me. There was also a man of the 7th Regiment named Nettleton, and one of the sailors, named Way, going in with their diarrhoea, so I had the prospect of company. My comrade had a pair of his regimental boots with him, but could not wear them in consequence of his sore legs, so he sold them on the road to this place to one of the sailors for two roubles; by the same token I must tell you how he got on with a pair of dragoon boots, but first I must tell you that there was a pair of spurs screwed in them and they were so rusted in they could not be got out. One day, and I believe the first day he wore them, he had to come down a flight of stairs out of a prison, and he forgot the spurs in the heels until they threw him headlong down the flight of stairs, but luckily did not hurt him much, and it was laughable to see how careful he was in future. For instance, if he had any steps or stairs to descend he would come down backwards. The money for those boots and what little I had came in very handy while in hospital.

We were received in the hospital about 7 o'clock, and the doctor came at 10. The hospital was solely for the use of the sick convicts, and there was a good lot of them there. It was a low, log building with only the ground floor. The door was at the back and in the centre of the house, and opened into a wide passage where there was a guard of soldiers. Four wards opened into this passage, each holding 20 men, and we were put in the farthest on the right. We had two windows facing the street and both were heavily barred, and two at the end in like condition. There was beds and bedsteads, and the place was warm and tolerably clean. The floor was painted brown and gave it a clean appearance. Each patient was supplied with a pair of slippers and cotton shirt, drawers and coat and night cap. There was no blankets to the beds, but two sheets (rather tough) and a heavy rug.

The doctor came to us first on his arrival, and ordered me to be bled immediately. The vein was opened by a lance in a case that worked with a spring, something like our cupping lances. The blood that came from me was quite black, and as soon as it began to flow I began to feel better. He took a good deal of blood from me. So much so, that I fell back on the bed in a faint and after into a deep sleep.

I was much better still when I awoke, but weak. The doctor had sent me some ointment for my face and lotion for my bruises, and some medicine. My comrade Farquharson had got permission from him for us to smoke, with the condition that we should go into the passage with the guard while we smoked. Also he gave him permission to go out to market for anything we required, which was a great favour.

On the first night one of the convicts died in one of the corners, and I took great interest in watching the old man nurse making illuminations round the body, chanting some low tune the while.

I had another attack of the toothache the next morning and, as soon as the doctor came, I made signs that I wanted it out. He seemed to be short of tools, for the only thing he could find likely to do the job were an old pair of wire nippers. He motioned me to sit down and got the old man nurse and a lump of a patient to hold my head. He got the tooth between the old nippers and without lancing the gums or making any preparation he set to work with all his might, pulling and shoving the tooth backwards and forwards until it had worked loose enough and then, with a strong sudden pull he fetched it out. The operation of pulling and shoving lasted better than ten minutes, and when he had finished he patted me on the back and appeared pleased that I could stand the pain so well without crying out.

Our diet was: for breakfast, one pint of thin soup and about two ounces of boiled beef or mutton; for dinner, ditto and for supper, ditto; a loaf of white bread, very good and weighing about a pound and a half daily, but we used to send out for bread, butter, honey, milk and tobacco. We also sent for a pack of cards and some writing paper and a pencil, and we amused ourselves greatly by writing down the names of many things so that we could read and learn them.

After supper we used to commence card playing and generally kept it up until 12 o'clock; then we would go to bed and sleep until breakfast time, walk about the ward—sleep, smoke and write through the day, and wind up playing cards at night. There was a convict in our room who told us he was a Pole and had been a soldier under Napoleon, had lost two of his fingers in some engagement, and was now a convict for making money (which I took to be coining, making counterfeit money). He could speak but very little French, but he learnt us several tricks on the cards, which served to pass away the time.

The first Wednesday we were there we were given to understand that, after dinner, we were to go for a wash. I was glad of it, for we had not had a wash since our entrance, and this is the only fault I have to find with the establishment. When the day came and dinner over, we were marched out of the house to another in the yard. The weather, since our entrance, had increased greatly in severity. It froze at the rate of 16 knots an hour—at least so the sailors said—and the snow was three feet deep. We crossed the yard in our cotton coats and drawers and was put in a room where we were told to strip, which we did.

When we were naked we entered another room, with a brick floor and the room was dreadfully warm. All around, and close up to the ceiling were long seats, and others below them on which the naked convicts hastened to seat themselves. In the middle of the room was a large copper, bottom upwards, and a large fire underneath. The copper was red hot in some places. In one corner of the room was two other coppers, right way up, and full of boiling water. An old woman was there making up the fires under the coppers and, when all her naked company were seated she took a bucket and commenced throwing the hot water on the red hot copper. The steam produced was stifling and the perspiration ran off me in streams. By continuing to apply the hot water to the copper the steam and heat increased and, for a time I felt as though I was suffocating, but gradully got the better of it. The convicts appeared to enjoy it vastly, but I was tired before we commenced properly. I went looking about for a tub that I might have a good wash, English fashion, and at last I found one and got some hot and cold water and had a tolerable wash. As soon as I had done I turned to the door to make my exit and, on the instant I turned I was doused with a bucket of cold water. I cannot describe the sensation this ducking caused me. I thought at first I was killed outright, and, as soon as I could, I turned round to chastise the person who had served me such a trick, and I found it was the doing of the old woman who stood grinning at me at a short distance. Had it been a man I would certainly have given him something for his trouble that would have astonished him. As it was I gave her a ferocious look and stalked out of the room in all my naked dignity. I took notice that the convicts, when they came out of the room ran and rolled themselves in the snow outside the building and enjoyed the change from oppressive heat to bitter cold. As soon as we were dressed the guard began to make us fall in outside the building in the snow, but, as I did not consider myself on the same footing as the convicts, I took to my heels and ran into the hospital, followed by the other three English. Several of the guard came after us and wanted to make us go out again to stand in the cold while we were numbered, but the doctor came in and put a stop to such nonsense.

The next day the doctor's son, a lad of twelve years of age, who used to spend the great part of his time with us English in asking the names of everything in English and writing it down (and we found him very handy to run errands for us to the market), brought a respectable dressed person, who told us he could speak French. I found that he was worse at it than myself, but I learned the name of the town from him, which was Walka, and I also learned the day of the month, which I was surprised to find was the 11th of January, and I could not help comparing my then present position with what it was that day twelvemonth when I was happy at home on furlough.

Nettleton of the 7th Regiment left hospital about this time and was sent on the road by himself to the next town. (I was in hospital on the first anniversary of your wedding, William, and I went through all the scenes of the day in my mind and many times wished you many happy returns of the day.)

> This was the 14th January 1855. Walka is probably Valka—the Russian for 'Ravine' and a very common village name in Southern Russia.

When Wednesday came again they wanted us to go to the bath once more; my two companions went, but I would not go, for I had not forgotten the dousing the old woman gave me. The next day they gave us to understand that we were to leave, but Way, the old sailor, was allowed the option of stopping as he was no better; but he did not relish the idea of being left by himself and so determined to come out with us. After the doctor's visit our clothes were brought to us and they must have been kept in some very cold place, for they were all as stiff as boards through frost, and the lice were completely done up for they had turned the colour of red gooseberries and were all dead. I was glad of this, and put on my old rags more willingly than I had for some time before, although they were so cold and stiff.

There were several convicts came out with us and a blacksmith was brought into the ward to rivet their leg irons afresh. The Pole, who had learned us the card tricks, was one of their number. We left the hospital about 11 o'clock and was marched to the prison where we were first put on our arrival in the town, but not in the same room, for, as there was but three of us, we were put in a rather large cell, plenty large enough to accommodate us. We had no money left and our first care was to apply for our pay.

After considerable bother we were informed that there was no pay coming to us for the day we came out of hospital, but, as we were to march the next morning and the next town was two days' journey off they gave us the pay for the two days' journey instead of giving it to us the next morning. As soon as we received it me and my little comrade Farquharson, the trumpeter, went to market. It was a small, miserable market place and very little exposed for sale. We managed to buy some dried French beans and a kind of bacon, common among the Russians, consisting of the fat of a pig cut off with the skin about an inch thick in square pieces weighing about two pounds each, but generally very rusty.

When we had cooked it we proceeded to satisfy our hunger and the old sailor, Way, always a great eater, put a good quantity out of sight and it did not agree with his stomach, for it was awfully rusty and he threw it up again, at the same time finding fault with our marketing. But soon after a woman came in bringing a roasted sucking pig and a dish of baked potatoes for which she wanted 15 copecks (6d English). We clubbed together and bought it and he made ample amends for the rusty bacon.

This night I could feel again the vermin running about me, shewing plainly that the prisons swarmed with them.

Early next morning a whole gang of convicts were assembled in the yard undergoing the operation of re-riveting their irons. About 6 o'clock, while it was still dark, we commenced our journey. There was four women among the convicts, one of whom had a child in her arms. There was an officer in charge of the party, but he did not interfere with us walking on ahead, but we could not now as formerly get much in front, because the snow was so deep, and made walking very hard work, and we were also in danger of losing the road if we got too far in advance of our party, as the whole country is covered with snow, which was drifting greatly this day and soon filled up all old tracks of sleighs. The weather was very severe, the snow and my breath froze upon my beard and formed icicles three or four inches long and completely fastened up my mouth so right to, that I could not get the end of my pipe into my mouth without first thawing or breaking the icicles, and obliged to break them caused much pain.

The day's march was a very long one, no less than 44 versts, a good day's march in fine weather, and a very fatiguing one in such weather as we had. The poor convicts suffered very much this day. Whenever we halted for a few minutes' rest they threw themselves down in the snow to ease their wearied limbs and many kicks would be bestowed on them to get them up when the order was given to proceed.

I saw one of the convict women publicly flogged this day. I don't know what she had done, but the officer ordered her to be flogged and a soldier soon gathered a rod from a willow tree by the roadside. They took her off the road to the end of an old shed, but quite exposed to the view of very many hands. My old curiosity was excited to see the punishment and, of course, I took up a position that would satisfy me. One of the soldiers (of whom there were plenty already) pressed her head down and held it between his legs. Another threw up her old sheepskin coat and apology for a pettycoat—and you must excuse my modesty for not describing all I saw on that very particular occasion. But the soldier with the rod laid on until the one who was counting the strokes called him to stop. The fellow used the rod with both hands and appeared to relish the job, and the other appeared to think it a bit of good fun, but I could plainly see that the unfortunate culprit did not think the operation very pleasant.

I don't know if my disgust was depicted in my countenance (as a novel writer would say) but she seemed to take a great liking to me afterwards and, if ever I was near the convicts after, she would run and place her arm through mine and talk at a great rate about something, but I could not understand her (but I have no doubt it was something about her flogging). She was a young woman, I should say not more than 24 years of age, and rather stout and good-looking.

We arrived at our halting place about 10 o'clock at night and were put in an old dilapidated roadside prison, the whole interior of which presented a very uncomfortable appearance. The place, like the others, was built with logs and the interstices had not been properly filled up, or rather, if they had, the stopping had fallen out and the fine drift snow penetrated through a hundred such places in different parts of the room. Large icicles hung from the straw thatched roof and the old cobwebs formed complete wreaths on which the frost glittered and sparkled like diamonds. The drift snow covered the earthen floor and, when the guard lighted a candle the whole place glittered in its frozen splendour.

The convicts lay down as soon as they entered, for they

were completely worn out, and I and my two companions, Farquharson and Way, kicked up a row with the sergeant for putting us in this place, and he took us to the guard house to stop among the soldiers. As the hour was late we could get nothing to eat but a few boiled beans off the soldiers, for which we had to pay through our noses (as the old saying has it). After our miserable supper we laid down to sleep and found to our great vexation that our sheepskin coats were wet through the frost and drift snow on the road and the warmth of our present lodging place. I awoke sometime during the night and found myself shivering with cold. The fire in the oven had gone out and the room was getting colder every minute. I tried to sleep again, but without success and at last I got up and tried to find a warmer place. I searched a long time before I could make out a warmer place. At last I perceived that the top of the oven was about a foot and a half from the ceiling and I managed to squeeze myself between the ceiling and top of the oven, but the place was not long enough for me and my legs hung over the side. I could not lay on my side and draw them up for the place was not high enough to allow of the height of my shoulders and I was obliged to lie on my back and my legs hanging down.

The bricks on top of the oven were still warm and I soon fell asleep. I was awakened again ere 'twas day break and had to get ready for the march. My legs ached terribly through the position I had taken on the oven.

In fact, this was a common practice among the Russian peasants. Madam Hommaire describes the procedure:

"Russian peasant stoves have flat tops on which they often sleep—sometimes with fatal results. They close the stoves before the usual time and lie down on them, for in the peasant houses the stoves are so constructed as to present a platform, on the top of which the family sleep in winter. On entering the cabin you see the inmates lying on their bellies, chatting pleasantly with one another. Their faces are tumid and a deep red hue, from the effects of the fumes."

CHAPTER SIX

Kharkov to Voronesh
20th January – 13th February

THE BATTLE OF INKERMAN.—REPULSE OF THE RUSSIANS

He got us some English newspapers ('The Illustrated London News') and I, for

We started off while it was yet dark and found the weather even worse than the day before. After 28 versts we came on the top of a hill and in a valley beneath and on a hill opposite stood the town of Karkoff, the largest and best town I saw in Russia.

> Kharkov, lying mainly on a plateau, was the capital of the government of the region of that area, which was known as 'Little Russia'. It had a University, founded in 1804 and was to become the centre of the iron and coal industry of South Russia. It had four great fairs.
>
> Newman and his party arrived here about the 20th January 1855.

We were marched a short distance down the main street and then turned to the left towards a large prison on the outskirts of the town. There were two prisons, one in the rear of the other. The convicts were put in the one in the rear for a time and they did not know what to do with us, for they sent us first to the front one then to the rear one and back again to the front one and then back again to the one in the rear, where the three of us were at last put into a long room with a long wooden guard bed reaching from end to end. We had not a copeck of money left and we were tremendous hungry, and the governor, coming in just after us, we asked him for money, telling him we had nothing to eat since 7 o'clock that morning and had no money to buy anything. Mr. Governor gave us to understand he could not help it and that we should have our pay in the morning when we commenced the march again, which he informed us would be on the morning after the morrow.

So here was a pretty look-out for us: the prospect of going without victuals the whole of the day, the whole of the next and part of the day after. You may be sure such a piece of intelligence caused a bit of grumbling and discontent, and I had just finished an eloquent oration, denouncing the whole Russian Government, from the Emperor down, when some person demanded, "What is the matter with you, country-men?" in good English.

We all turned and found a respectably dressed man wearing spectacles, standing in the doorway. To our many questions he told us that he was an Englishman and was a professor of foreign languages and was living with a Russian nobleman in this town, of the name of Alexis. After some more talk he said he would give us enough to provide us with a supper and would try and get us removed to the other prison, where, he informed us, there was several other English prisoners. He gave me a twenty and fifteen copeck piece and soon had us shifted to the other prison, where we were put in a tolerable room, but rather scant of furniture (as it had only a table and two forms) but it had the appearance of being clean.

There was another room, a moderate sized one opened from the one we occupied and here we found the man of the 7th named Nettleton who had left us in the hospital and McDonell who killed the pig and soldier. He had been ill and left behind in the prison hospital and had only this day left it. There was a private of the 11th Hussars, named Henry, cutting a dash with his cherry coloured trowsers and frogged jacket, and McCartney, a clerk or issuer of the Commissariat; both had been taken at Balaclava, but I never could make out how the commissary man got mixed up in that affair. He had given in his rank as an officer when taken and was treated accordingly; he received 75 copecks per diem and was allowed a sleigh to himself, and at night a separate billet.

The 11th Hussars, famous as the 'Cherry Pickers' from the colour of their overalls, were in the second rank in the charge at Balaclava. One of their officers, Sir Roger Palmer, told the following story:

"A few nights before Balaclava I was orderly Officer and, going the rounds at night, found Private Jowett of my troop sitting down (I am afraid) asleep at his post. I did not know what to do, as he was one of the best men in the troop. While I was thinking, the Orderly Sergeant Major said to me, in a dictatorial tone of voice 'You must confine him, sir, or the Colonel will be very angry.'

"This determined me. I turned to the Sgt. Major and said 'What the devil do you mean by daring to speak to me like that? If you say another word I will put you under arrest for insolence to a superior officer.'

"After cautioning Jowett not to sit down at his post again I left him.

"In the evening after the battle, I was talking to Lt. Dunne and he said to me 'You had a very near shave today, old fellow, as, while we were rallying, a Russian came up behind you and put up his carbine to your head. You did not see him, but Private Jowett charged him and cut him down.' "

There was also one of the sailors still sick in the prison, and two Italian sailors, who I know nothing of except that they were there. Their room was pretty well furnished, each man having a bed, and there was a table and several chairs and a tea urn and a set of chinz tea things. I observed three nice ribs of beef and a score or more of French rolls in one of the windows, together with some cold ham and plenty of butter, cheese, tea and sugar. I fully expected, on finding such a stock of the good things of this life in possession of an Englishman (and those Englishmen brother soldiers and fellow prisoners of war), that we should have been invited to have some of it, especially as Nettleton had been kept in extra victuals by my comrade and me while he was in hospital; but although they could not help seeing that we wanted it badly, they never so much as enquired if we had had anything to eat during the day, and McDonell told us that he had come out of hospital that morning and was in the room (our room) walking about while they got their breakfast, and the same at dinner, and they well knew he had neither victuals, nor a copper of money to buy any and yet they never asked him to have a morsel.

He also told us that the provisions were supplied daily from the nobleman's house where our first visitor lived, and that the three of them (McCartney, Nettleton and Henry) went every day to dine with the nobleman, and that a fine sleigh, with two fine horses, drove up to the prison every evening to take them to the nobleman's house. The two Italians also had some good friends in the town, who used to provide them with everything they required, and drove up to the prison each night to take them to their house. I soon found all this to be true and more besides.

Me and my comrade, Farquharson went to market and bought some mutton and bread and onions, with which, upon our return, the old sailor, Way, knocked up a very good mess. Before it was ready, however, I observed the three favourites getting ready for tea. I saw the table laid with many good things and the urn hissing in the midst. But when they were going to begin they actually closed the door, as I supposed for fear any of us should make ourselves so bold as to intrude upon them. I was much vexed by such treatment by men in captivity like myself, but I scorned to say anything about it.

When our mess was ready we set to in earnest, inviting McDonell to assist us, and we soon polished the whole. Just as we were beginning a liveried servant came in and said something to Henry, upon which the trio set off with him in the sleigh to the nobleman's dinner. A few minutes after the Italians went also and we were left to ourselves. We were yet eating when in came two ladies who stood and looked at us eating for some time. I could find that they were French, but I did not speak to them as I was so pleasantly engaged. They went into the other room, but, finding the birds had flown, took their departure.

Soon after they were gone, a grey haired middle-aged man came and soon let us know he was a schoolmaster (and an English one, too). He was a curious character and sat with us some time, telling us many anecdotes of the Russians, among whom he had lived for a long time. He got us some English newspapers (the 'Illustrated London News') and I, for the the first time, found out the name of the battle in which I was taken prisoner. There was an engraving of the fight and a list of the killed and wounded, which interested me very much. But I noticed whole paragraphs and articles were effaced or thoroughly cut out, and that only left that did not offend the sensitive feelings of the Russians.

Among other things the old schoolmaster advised us strongly against habituating ourselves to drinking Walki, and when we did drink a glass of it always to swallow two or three mouthfuls of water previous to the spirit, for he assured us it was a most killing drink in the whole universe. Also he told us that a report had been sent to the Governor of the district about the killing of one of our escort, and he advised that whenever an officer, or any other of our escort, or any person used us badly, to write a note detailing the circumstance and direct it to the Emperor at St. Petersburgh, and give it to the officer commanding or in charge of us; adding that it would frighten an officer into treating us civilly, more especially those who had risen through the ranks and who, he said, had generally the duty to take charge of convoys. We tried this plan once or twice afterwards and found it answered very well. The sight

REPULSE OF THE RUSSIANS BY THE 2ND DIVISION

The annexed Engraving (from a Sketch taken by an eye-witness) gives a faithful representation of what might be seen in one part of the field about ten o'clock on the memorable 5th of November.   On the hill-side, in the background, may be seen the ruins of the ancient town of Inkerman, from which the battle has taken its name. A large body of Russians are ascending the heights in close column—having been ordered by the Imperial Archdukes, to drive the Allies into the sea—and are met with a charge of bayonets by the Second Division, which fought so bravely, and suffered so severely, in that desperate engagement.

Prince Menschikoff, in his apologetic description of the battle, ascribes his repulse to the fact that the Russian Commanders were wounded; and that "the enemy's infantry occasioned great losses in horses, artillerymen, and infantry officers."   A more just explanation would have been to confess that the wretched serfs, raised on black bread and quass, whom the Czar sends him, are unable to stand against English and French soldiers, even when the former number more than four to one of the latter.

The regiments belonging to the Second Division, which took so prominent a part in that day's engagement, were the 30th, 41st, 47th, 49th, 55th and 95th.   In these six regiments alone, 9 officers and 179 rank and file were killed; and 22 officers and 447 men were wounded.   We have no means of ascertaining what loss the Second Division inflicted on the enemy, but there is no doubt that they performed their full share of the terrible work of that day.

The following description of one portion of the battle by an eye-witness gives some notion of the scene which must have presented itself to a spectator an hour or two before noon on the heights opposite Inkerman:—

The enemy were now completely out of the bush which had screened and sheltered them on their advance, and upon fair ground they stood no chance with our men. Our regiments halted, extended their line to the left, and commenced a tremendous file fire.   The enemy, in disorder, hardly returned a shot, but stood their ground, and fell by hundreds and hundreds.   Thrice they moved up stolidly to break our line on the left, and were met each time by terrible volleys of musketry, until they closed in, when our fellows charged and massacred them at the point of the bayonet.   The fortune of the day still hung doubtful.   The enemy were getting up all their strength for a final effort, when Canrobert came up with three regiments of Zouaves, five regiments of French infantry, and a strong force of artillery, and commenced a terrible attack on the enemy's right flank.

This occurred about eleven o'clock, and from that moment the Russian chance was hopeless.   Yet, though under the French fire they were literally falling by battalions, they never showed the least sign of trepidation or disorder.   On the contrary, they formed up in the most beautiful order, altered their front so as to meet the attack of the French, and, extending their line to the left, prepared to resume their attack upon the English.   At that time, however, our men were well prepared, and, without any order or arrangement, flung themselves headlong upon the enemy, charging with the bayonet, which the enemy met for the first time.   The Russians now boldly charged with the bayonet also, and for the space of five minutes the 30th, 41st, 49th, 88th, and six or seven Russian regiments were stabbing, le[..]ting, and firing at each other in the most fearful manner.   At last the enemy gave way, and began retiring in good order across towards the Inkerman heights.   Until I saw it, I never in my life could have believed that any tropps in the world could have retired under such a murderous fire in such perfect order.   The French and English, with a whole mass of artillery followed close upon the retreating battalions, pouring in volley after volley of grapeshot, shell, and musketry.   In fact it was a perfect carnage.   Yet, in spite of this, the enemy kept their order, retreating almost at slow time, and every five or ten minutes halting and charging desperately up the hill at our men and the French. In these charges the Russians lost fearfully.   We received them with volleys of musketry, and then dashed at them with the bayonet.

of the writing and the magic words 'Emperor, St. Petersburgh' was sufficient to obtain all we required.

The old schoolmaster stopped with us a long time, and, before he left, he got us a large piece of felt to lie on and to cover us. In the middle of the night the trio returned, and told us a great tale: that they had been to the theatre, and were in one box, and the two Grand Dukes, Michael and Nicholas were there (the same two who had such a laugh at the soup report), and Henry the Hussar invited Farquharson to go with them on the next night. I nudged my companion not to accept the invitation after their neglect and unmannerly behaviour, but he did not appear to take the hint and closed with the invitation. The next morning we were again without provisions and money and did not know what to do for breakfast. The Governor came about 10 o'clock and we tackled him again for our pay, but with the same success. He went into the next room where the trio were at breakfast off cold ham, cold roast beef, French rolls and butter and tea, and they invited him to have a cup (making good the old law 'offer to those who don't require assistance'). While he was there the two French ladies came in, who had taken such interest in seeing us eat the night before. They also went into the little room and soon after the Italians' friends came in, who also went into the other room.

I was walking up and down our room in no very contented humour at the prospect of us going without victuals all day, when the two French ladies came out and were passing me on their road to the door, when I touched one of them on the arm, and asked her to speak to the Governor for us for our pay, and telling her as well as I could how we were situated. She appeared much pleased that I understood French, and poured question upon question until she had gained all the news of our condition. She then (aided by her companion) laid seige to the Governor, and I could see by her gesticulation that she was laying down the law very forcibly. But 'twas all of no use, for at last she came and told me we could not get our pay before the morrow morning, when we were to march, but added, in a low voice, that she would provide us with provisions during our stay and would be back with us by 11 o'clock. She then enquired our number and took off her glove to shake hands with me, assuring me at the same time that she would be back by 11 o'clock.

I was rather ashamed of the whole job now for I fancied it looked like begging, but nothing was farther from my thoughts at the time I spoke to her and had she had a less sweet voice, or had she been less young and pretty I think I should have haughtily declined her kind offer; but could offer no resistance to her, as she was, and therefore she had full scope for her hospitality, and nobly and kindly did she behave to us.

She was true to her time and brought us as much as would serve us for two days. She brought us about 20 French rolls, about 5 pounds of cheese, 2 very large and long German sausages, some cold roast beef and mutton, and a pound of tea, and five or six pounds of lump sugar. She promised to come in the evening and bring us some more, although I repeatedly told her we had plenty. She did not stop long, and as soon as she was gone we commenced our breakfast, and sent some of it and half the tea and sugar to the sick sailor in hospital.

While we were eating, the same person who had given us the money for supper the night before, came in, and whose name I now recollect was Eldridge. He enquired where we had gotten our supply of provisions from, and, upon my telling him 'From a French Lady' he seemed quite vexed and said he thought there was enough provisions in the next room to satisfy the whole of us. I replied that I did not doubt it in the least but those who had it took care to keep it. He left us in anything but a pleasant humour, but I could not see the reason he should be so offended to find us so well provided for.

During the course of the day I had my beard and whiskers shaved off, a job I soon repented when we began to march again. In the evening the trio and my comrade started off to the nobleman's house, and the Italians soon after also took their departure, and there was but three of us left, viz: myself, the old sailor, Way, and McDonell of the 41st.

Soon after they were gone the old schoolmaster came in and we had a long talking match. He was much pleased at McDonell's account of being taken, which was that he (McDonell) and another man of his regiment had been attacked by four Russians in the battle of Inkerman. Mcdonell shot one and his comrade bayonetted another, and the other two laid down their arms and surrendered, and each of the visitors took one of the survivors prisoner; but the man who had been bayonetted levelled his piece at McDonell's comrade and shot him dead. McDonell then put a finish to him with the butt of his piece and took charge of both the prisoners and marched them off, as he thought, among our own people; but was astonished to find that he had marched them into a large body of the enemy, where he soon was made to change places with the two Russians. The story pleased the old schoolmaster much, especially as McDonell was very young, though tall: in fact he was but a lad.

Inkerman has been called 'The Soldiers' Battle' because it was won, not by Generals throwing in great regiments at precisely the right moment, but by the initiative and determination of small groups, often fighting almost alone.

Every regiment involved has its own heroic tale to tell. At a light defence called the Sandbag Battery, the 41st were engaged in heavy fighting. Lt. Taylor, firing his revolver until it was empty, drew his sword and engaged a Russian officer. The others, British and Russian alike, drew aside, stopped fighting and formed up round the two contestants.

Each officer ran the other through at the same moment and died like medieval heroes.

About 9 o'clock the French lady came, but the schoolmaster had gone to try to persuade the Governor to allow us some straw beds. When she came in, she did not know me at first, through the disappearance of my beard, and laughed at the change when I spoke to her. She asked me to get my coat, and something else, which I did not understand. But, at last she went into the little room and brought a table cloth, and then took hold of my arm and led me down the stairs to the gates of the prison, where I found a two-horse sleigh, with the other lady in it. She made me hold the cloth by the corners, while she proceeded to fill it with French rolls, German sausages, black puddings, cheese, tea and sugar. She then took a pot from the sleigh, tied in a large white cloth which she carried herself, and the other lady brought a small hand basket, and we proceeded to our quarters.

When we got in she proceeded to lay out the table, and we found that the pot in the white cloth contained some beautiful, hot soup. She was rather puzzled for a moment, for she could not find any basins or soup plates for us to eat from, but she soon got some small wooden dishes from some woman of the prison. The other lady produced two bottles of wine and some glasses from the basket, and we had to sit down to the operations, for they said the soup would be spoilt if not eaten while warm. We were not hungry but could not refuse to gratify her and, after testing the soup, we liked it so much that we ate as much as though we had just come off a long march.

When we had finished, she cleared up the table and brought forward the wine and filled the glasses herself. She brought a couple of chairs and sat down with us, and many was the questions she put to me, some of which I could not understand at all, and others but partly; but the old schoolmaster came and soon satisfied all her questions. She asked me how many shirts we had each and whether we had any flannel for our chests, and then asked for one of our caps to inspect it. She was pleased at the manner in which we had tried to preserve our ears against Jack Frost, but she said the caps were not warm enough, as the weather would be colder the farther we got up the country, and she promised to come and see us before we started next morning and would bring some things with her.

The old schoolmaster related the story of how McDonell was taken and the ladies were highly pleased at it. When we told her we had all come out of hospital a day or two previous, she said it was cruel to make us march again so soon and she would try and get leave for us to stop for a week from the Governor of the town, and if she succeeded she would keep us while we remained, and we must come to her house to pass the evenings. She told us her name, which was Madame Tomasin. She stopped with us until past 11 o'clock, and then both the ladies and the schoolmaster went away together and the room did not appear the same after their departure.

We got the piece of felt to sleep on again and was soon fast asleep. Farquharson the trumpeter came in during the night, and next morning was made to stop in this town for some time. It appeared that he had been well treated and, being a good musician, the nobleman was pleased with him and promised to procure liberty from the Governor of the town for him to stop.

All hands, except the Italians, were to march this morning, but Henry the Hussar laid in bed and declared he was ill, though he had a queer look for a sick man; but I soon found out that him and Mr. Eldridge were combined to attempt to procure a longer stay, and I believe the Governor of the prison was also in co. with them. My comrade wanted to come upon the same plan, but without success. Madame Tomasin came about 8 o'clock and brought us some caps with soft warm ear pieces to them, also some pieces of different pattern cloth, thickly wadded and lined with silk, with four strings to tie them round the neck and waist, and the whole formed a comfortable chest warmer, in shape like a dicky. She also brought us some gloves, and then went away to the Governor to try for liberty for us to remain.

About 10 o'clock we were marched down to the other prison. McCartney and Nettleton being with us but Henry, feigning sickness, was left behind. At the other prison we were served out with a pair of gloves and our pay for the march, but my comrade would not take his pay, declaring he was ill and could not march. We here found two English ladies waiting to see us, whose names I forget. One was a middle-aged motherly-looking woman and the other was a good-looking young woman—and a parrot for talking. The younger was governess at the Governor's, and told us that she knew he would not consent for us to stop in the town any longer.

They gave us some shirts, stockings, gloves and bags to carry our victuals in. They also produced needles and thread and set to work to sew the earpieces on our caps tighter, and the strings on our breastplates. They remained with us during the time we stopped, and told us that there was several English and French ladies in the town and that they had formed a society to relieve the prisoners of each country as they passed through the town. They both spoke of Madame Tomasin in high terms. The elder lady's name I now recall was Harvey, but I cannot remember the name of the younger one—yet—yes I can—it was Miss Hardcastle. She told me that the main body of my party stopped 4 days in the town, and that there had been a great deal of linen and other things distributed among them; and that one of the French had made a sonnet upon the ladies of Karkoff and had given it to Madame

Tomasin, who immediately got it printed and sent copies of it to the different ladies; and the result was a munificent collection for the poet.

The ladies also kept up a correspondence with England, and regular notices appeared in *The Times* newspaper reporting the passage of officers through the town. On the 16th May 1855 Sgt. Newman's officer, Lt. Duff, passed through and this was duly reported in *The Times* on 5th June 1855.

Madame Tomasin now came in from her interview with the Governor of the town, and told us that she could not prevail on him to allow us to stop. She appeared sorry that she had failed in her attempt, but gave us each a 20 copeck piece and advised us strongly against Walki drinking. She also gave us some pipes and tobacco.

At last we were turned out to begin our march, and were obliged to bid farewell to our kind friends, Madame Tomasin assuring us that we should soon be through the town again on our way back to England, and inviting us to visit her when we did come. She drove off in her sleigh. The two other ladies remained with us until we got word to march, and then waved their kerchiefs in adieu.

We were a long time passing through the town—for it was very large and had plenty of spectators. After some time I felt inclined for a smoke and filled my pipe with some of Madame Tomasin's Turkish tobacco, and placed it in my mouth, while I proceeded to strike a light with a flint and steel, when a respectable citizen coolly knocked the pipe out of my mouth. I took this as a determined insult and soon began to put myself into shape to return the compliment, when he pointed to a large church we were passing and gave me to understand that I must not smoke near their churches again. But in most towns, as I afterwards learnt, they would not allow smoking outside the houses at all, quite the contrary to our country, where generally tobacco smoke is an abomination inside a house.

We travelled only 14 versts this day and were put in billets at night. I forgot to mention that, on starting this day, we were joined by three Austrian soldiers, prisoners like ourselves. They were all cavalry and wore their spurs. One of them was very ill in the waggon, another a short ugly fellow, but the third was a tall good-looking fellow. They were much displeased to find that we received 20 copecks per diem, and they only nine. My little comrade Farquharson, through not taking his pay this morning when offered, had to come away without any, for the clerk swore he had paid him; but it did not matter much as madame's benevolence had supplied us with plenty of provisions.

On reaching our billets we tried to bargain for a sucking pig, but the old woman wanted too much for it and would not make a fire for us to cook by, although we offered to pay for it; but at length we prevailed on her to get the urn filled with water and boiled, and we made our supper off one of Madame Tomasin's German sausages. During the time we were eating, one of the Austrians got some Walki (they were all billeted with us) and began drinking. We invited the two to supper who were not ill, which invitation they accepted and soon made three or four of our rolls disappear with a tollerable portion of sausage. After they had finished eating they commenced drinking again and pouring the Walki down the sick man's throat. I interfered and had to threaten the tall fellow with condign punishment if he persisted in so doing.

I then got a wet cloth and spread it on the sick man's temples and made him some more tea and put a jug of it in the oven to keep warm for him during the night. I got up several times during the night to re-wet the cloth and give him some tea, and in the morning had the satisfaction of finding him much better.

We started again about 8 o'clock, after some more tea and sausage, and reached our halting place about six p.m. We found out that the Austrians had been taken off picket by some Cossacks, though I could never make out where. The weather was bitter cold and we found our caps and breastplates very servicable. I had a good deal of talk with McCartney and found him a very intelligent man. He had been a sergeant in the Dublin police force.

We now began to have every third day off as a rest day, for the benefit of the convicts, of whom we picked up some fresh ones at each town, and our party gradually got stronger.

There was nothing occurred until we reached the town of Belguratt, a large town in a valley 250 versts from Karkoff. As we entered this town our drummer commenced rattling away to call all hands to look at us, and we soon had a good crowd round us. I noticed a large convent of sisters of mercy as we entered the town and many of the sisters of mercy came to look at us.

Belgorod, on the right bank of the Donetz, is a sizeable town, nestling below limestone cliffs.

We were all marched to a large prison, and the convicts were put in a large room and the Austrians with them. We English were marched to the other side of the yard and placed in a very large cell, and McCartney and Nettleton, who acted as his servant, was put in a similar one close to us. I was the first who entered the cell pointed out for our use, and was astonished to find two tall men wrapped in large cavalry red cloaks, standing inside. They soon introduced themselves as two of the 4th Heavy Dragoons. One's name was Donohoe and the other Joe Chapman. They had been taken off an outlying picket at Balaclava, long before the battle, and were the first prisoners the Russians took, except stragglers, when on our march from the place where we landed to Sebastopol.

Being both very tall, fine-looking men and well clothed, they attracted a great deal of notice from the Russians and had been treated like princes. They had had a great deal of money given them; so much that they could afford to treat the whole of the guard and the convicts on the road daily, and generally made the guard drunk at night. They had managed to drink themselves into a fever and the delirium tremens, and had been in this prison hospital about two months and had only come out this evening. Of course there was a great deal to talk of, and the battles of Balaclava and Inkerman to tell of, and we had to send for a bottle of the crayture to assist our memories.

The 4th (Royal Irish) Dragoon Guards were commanded during the Crimean War by Col. Edward Hodge, whose letters home have been edited and published under the title of 'Little Hodge'.

On the 17th October, Privates Driscoll, Chapman and Donoghue (Donohoe) were taken prisoner by Cossacks, while on patrol duty. Driscoll and Chapman, as recorded by Col. Hodge, returned from captivity, but Donoghue died in captivity, as later recalled by Newman.

I was the cook, as usual, and soon made a fine potful of soup and boiled another of murphies. We all had a good hearty supper. The Heavies declared that they had not tasted such a good mess since they left Old England. After supper McCartney came in and he and Donohoe were soon thick friends and McCartney invited Donohoe out to a tea drinking shop to have some tea. Donohoe, although he was so weak he could scarcely stand, agreed, and put the bottle in his pocket, determined to bring some more Walki. They were gone about an hour and a half, and returned bearing convincing proof of the strength of the 'tea' they had been drinking. The bottle was produced and soon emptied, and Donohoe persuaded Chapman to go and fetch more. Joe consented, and I inwardly wished that something would happen to stop the drinking, for I was very tired and wanted to rest. Joe got the bottle filled and returned, but in coming through the gate the bottle dropped from under his cloak and the sentry picked it up and gave it to the Sgt. of the Guard. Joe and Donohoe tried all they knew to get the bottle back again, but without effect and, at last, to my joy, laid down to sleep.

We remained here all the next day, and in the morning we bought some nice beef; but the old man who had charge of us threw many obstacles in our way to hinder us in our cooking. I knew he wanted us to pay him to get it done, but we determined not to let him have a copeck out of us. So we could not get to cook in the cook house. Donohoe and me stole wood and made a fire in our own room and cooked there.

There was nothing particular occurred this day, except that we got our shirts washed by some of the women prisoners for three copecks each.

The next day we resumed our march. Donohoe and Chapman, being unable to march, were placed in a sleigh, wrapped up in their cloaks and sheepskins. The Austrians took another road from this town and we saw them no more. The sick man had quite recovered before we reached this town. We started about 10 o'clock and had a long day's march, and Donohoe and Joe would call at every dram shop; but it was rather excusable, for they were nearly frozen to death through sitting in a sleigh all day in such weather.

There was now eight of us English, Donohoe, Chapman, Farquharson, McCartney, Nettleton, the old sailor Way, McDonell of the 41st and me. We had a pretty tolerable lodging, but, to our vexation, found out next day that the lice were collecting again in great force; but we adopted a new plan with the gentlemen, and turned our trowsers inside out before we started and they soon froze to death when we got upon the road. They always turned red with the frost and would fall off when dead: a capital plan of taking them nasty and one we often practiced after finding the benefit of the first trial. We even, sometimes, went so far in our method of vengeance that we would wear our shirts outside, or take them off and hang them outside upon our arrival in our billets, and we soon diminished their numbers.

One night on this march we got into a billet where the old man and woman and the whole of the family tried to make us as uncomfortable as possible. They would sell us no provisions, and, where we had bought a goose and potatoes at another house, they would neither light a fire not let us cook by one of our own making: a proceeding that brought forth many angry ejaculations from Donohoe. We tried to coax them, we offered them double the money we were in the habit of giving for such things, but they continued obdurate and would not accommodate us. At length Donohoe jumped up and seized a large picture of the Virgin and another of some other saint, and seizing an old chopper, he began to split them up, swearing he would have a fire. There was a great rush immediately by all the various members of the household to rescue their Gods, but Donohoe brandished the chopper and, though they liked their saints well, yet they shewed that they liked themselves too well to endanger a broken head for their patrons.

At length a compromise was made, that Donohoe should give up the pictures and they should make a fire, which was soon done after the restoration of the saints to their posts of honour, and we eventually got our supper cooked for us and plenty of straw brought to lie on. In fact they appeared to think they could not do too much to keep good friends with such barbarians. I was glad the job was settled so amicably, for we were but five and had a row commenced we should undoubtedly have got the worst of it.

The next morning their civility increased rather than diminished and, upon our asking for milk, the old woman went out to find some for us among her neighbours, and make it hot for us afterwards. After we had left the house to resume our march I went back for my stick, which I had forgotten, and there found the whole family bowing and scraping and crossing before the pictures (doubtless in thanksgiving for our departure).

We arrived in a small town this evening, but I forget the name of it, though I rather think it was Voleski.

Probably Voluyki, east south east of Belgorod.

We were put into a small prison and had the warders' room allotted to us, and McCartney and Nettleton. We had scarcely got in when a woman came and offered for sale two roast geese and two large dishes of baked potatoes for 30 copecks, which we soon bought and demolished. We stopped here the whole of the succeeding day and had a Russian prisoner of some note placed with us. He assured McCartney (who spoke the most Russian) that the Government had taken as many as three million roubles from him, which he had made by smuggling. He was allowed 75 copecks per diem and a sleigh to himself, a separate apartment in prison and a convict as a servant. He was a good scholar and understood arithmetic well.

The next morning McCartney reported himself sick and was left behind, and Nettleton with him.

On the march we had in addition to the convict smuggler, a convict priest who, from what we could learn, had, by some wonderful process, got a young woman with child; and when the youngster was brought forth into this vale of tears, he thoughtfully determined that its suffering should be short but warm, and threw it on a large fire, which soon made an end to it as far as this life was concerned. But the mother's mother reported the circumstances. There was something difficult in the circumstances and thus he was not hung or beheaded, but transported to Siberia.

Madame Hommaire, in a colourful condemnation of the Russian priesthood:

"Nothing can exceed the depravity of the Russian clergy; their ignorance is on a par with their vicious propensities. Most of the monks and priests pass their lives in disgraceful intoxication that renders them incapable of decently discharging their religious duties. The priestly office is regarded in Russia, not as a sacred calling, but as a means of escaping from slavery and attaining nobility. The monks, deacons and priests that swarm in the churches and monasteries, are almost all sons of the peasants who have entered the church, that they may no longer be liable to the misfortune of being made soldiers. But though they thereby acquire the right to plunder the serfs, and catechise them after their own fashion, they cannot efface the stain of their birth, and they continue to be regarded by the nobility with that sovereign disdain which the latter profess for all who are not sprung from their own caste. The great and petty nobles are perfectly agreed in this respect, and it is not uncommon to see a pometshik raise his hand to strike a pope, whilst the latter humbly bows his head to receive the chastisement. This resignation, which would be exemplary if it were to be ascribed to evangelical humility, is here but the result of the base and crouching character of the slave, of which the Russian priest cannot divest himself, even in the midst of the highest functions of his spiritual life."

In 1854 the total population of Russia was about 61,000,000 of whom about 550,000 were clergy or their families; 16,000,000 were 'nobility' and bourgoisie, and no fewer than 45,000,000, or 73 per cent of the population, serfs.

This figure can, however, be somewhat misleading, as the serfs were either crown serfs and virtually freemen,

tilling their land leased to them by the crown, or seignio-
rial serfs, who were serfs in the true sense, being owned
with the land. They were expected to work half the week
for their master and allowed to till the small piece of land
leased to them, during the rest of the time. Should they
indulge in craft or industry the proceeds had to go to
their masters. All hawkers and pedlars were slaves, making
useful incomes for their masters.

Serfs could only marry with the consent of their lord,
who delegated this to his steward, whose sole object in
this field was the rapid increase of the population. Unions
were usually arranged at an early age, as the price of a
family could range from £25 to £40.

Military service, for which the serfs were liable, was a
source of constant anxiety. When it was necessary to raise
more troops, the instruction was sent to the head man of
the village in crown lands and the Steward in private
lands, to select the future heroes, who were then fettered
to prevent their escape.

At the start of the Crimean War a rumour was rife
that those serfs who volunteered for military service would
be given their freedom. This was totally untrue and
caused great embarrassment, as the thousands of volunteers had to be returned to their villages.

This day was very cold and at night we were placed in a
roadside prison, and the officer in charge of us had an inspection
of all the things we had been served with by the government,
for what purpose I don't know. A clean dressed civilian here
asked the officer to allow us to stop at his house, which, after
some squabbling with us, he agreed to. We found that we were
only wanted to be looked at by a whole lot of peasants, which
investigation did not suit McDonell, who soon cleared the
apartment allotted to us of all the spectators.

The next day our officer ordered four of the women of the convicts to be ironed by the wrists and chained together like the men. I don't know what they had done, but his orders were soon obeyed, and, as the women could not now put their hands inside their sheepskins, they were soon frostbitten, for they had no gloves. After an hour's marching they begged and cried him to take the irons off, but he kept them on half the day.

In the afternoon one of the convicts fell down in a fit and, by the officer's orders, the guards commenced kicking and striking him with their firelocks to make him get up. My little comrade Farquharson was near getting himself into trouble through interfering, for he did not like to see the poor fellow so ill used for being afflicted. They belaboured him so much that he could not march when he came to his senses, and they were obliged to put him on one of the sleighs.

During this march my comrade laid his money bag out of his hand in the billet one evening, and it was immediately stolen, so that we got upon short rations before the journey was completed.

At last, one evening, we were informed that we must march the next morning at 4 o'clock and that we had 45 versts to go to the town where we were to halt. We were woke very early by the guard and, with a very meagre breakfast, we turned out. I never experienced such a cold, bitter day. The wind penetrated through my old clothing and large icicles collected on my moustache and beard, from my breath from my nostrils. The snow was above our knees and hard at the top so that it cut our legs severely. The darkness made it more disagreeable still, and I was never so miserable before.

We were obliged to march with the convicts until daybreak, for we could not see our road. The old sailor, Way, had his nose shockingly frostbitten, and also several of the guard. Donohoe and Chapman could not stand riding, and were glad to get out and walk.

About 11 o'clock we came to some houses by the roadside, and found a lad who spoke broken English and invited us into the house. The convicts were to halt here for an hour's rest and a fresh relief of sleighs, so we went in and found an old grey-headed man who could speak a little French, and he invited us to have some tea. The urn was already boiling and we were soon supplied with tumblers of tea. The old fellow then invited us to have some roast goose, to which we assented, and a goose soon made its appearance on the table and was soon converted into a skeleton.

The old man appeared much pleased with his guests and caught hold of the old sailor and kissed him, to our amusement and his indignation.

At length the word was given to start again and we rose to leave, when, guess our astonishment at the charge of 30 copecks each for our feeding. Donohoe, in his rage at being caught in such a trap, caught the skeleton of the goose and hurled it at the old man's head, and would doubtless have gone on to more serious acts of disturbance only that the officer of the escort was sitting in the room and had been watching the whole concern. We were obliged to pay and those who had money were obliged to stump out for those who had none, and some had but very little as this was the last day of our pay. However, we managed to pay and laughed at the dodge the old man had played us to ensure our custom, and the old sailor, Way, was joked for a long time about the kissing match (and we found out soon afterwards that the old man and the lad had taken the main body of our party in in the same manner and several others who came up after us).

We reached a large town called Starriosko about 5 p.m. and were put in a large prison in the gaoler's room.

Starry Oskol, north east of Belgorod.

I was much struck by the great quantity of pigeons and

jackdaws in the town. The cornices of the buildings and churches were completely black with them, and I saw them in the street by the hundreds together; and they did not attempt to fly away upon the approach of any person but would merely hop out of the way. The Russians regard these birds as holy and will not hurt them.

Upon our arrival in the prison Donohoe, being the most moneyed man, advanced half a rouble to get provisions, and I and McDonell went to market. There was not much to be bought as most of the market was closed, but I managed to buy a whole leg of fresh pork, some bread and onions and pepper and salt. When I returned to the prison, Donohoe grumbled at the fare I had provided and said he had never heard of fresh pork soup; but I did not mind his grumbling, but began to get ready for cooking.

I and the old sailor had a tremendous job to get the leg of pork into pieces, for it was frozen as hard as a log and it was hard work to get a sharp axe into it. When it was cooked Donohoe altered his tone and declared it was excellent, and we made a good supper.

We had some person come to visit us who, upon his entrance, asked if any of us could speak French. I told him that I could, a little, and he went on to tell me that he was an Italian dancing master, and he should like us to come to his house to pass the evening, and that he would go and ask the Governor's permission for us to go; but, as he was speaking, the Governor came in and he asked and was granted the necessary permission. He then said he would go and let his people know we were coming, and would come back for us. He went away, but did not return, and we were not surprised for we all thought he was trying to shirk out of his promise.

My little comrade Farquharson complained of being unwell this night and also was so ill the next morning that we had to leave him behind. During the day's march we came to a river frozen to a great depth and we continued the journey on ice.

This was the great River Don.

We got to a little village by 6 o'clock and were billeted. After we had supped a soldier came up and told the two heavies that the officer wanted them. They accordingly went and, after, the soldier came back and beckoned me to follow him. He conducted me to the house where the officer stopped. I was ushered into a large room where I found the officer seated at tea with a lady, and the heavies were taking tea very comfortably with them. I soon found that I had been sent for to parlay with the lady, who could speak French well. I had just finished the second tumbler of tea and the lady and two or three domestics were clearing the table of the tea apparatus and supplying its place with decanters and glasses, and I had made up my mind for a comfortable evening, especially as the lady began twanging the strings of a guitar, when we heard the sound of sleigh bells stop in front of the house and directly after a tall officer with clanking sword strode into the apartment.

He stared at us for some moments and appeared to be perfectly astonished at our appearance and apparent composure. He demanded of our officer in an authoriative voice what we were and what we were doing there. Our officer muttered something in reply and took off his cap to the other, but Mr. Consequence called aloud for the soldiers and the room was soon filled with them and he ordered them to march us back to our billets.

The lady told him I could speak a little French and she had sent for us to have a little talk with me. Upon this he called me back and asked me my name, but, as I had no great opinion of him, I told him it did not matter to him, upon which he informed me in a rage that he was an officer and would have me flogged. I replied that if he did I would write to the Emperor tomorrow and tell him of the circumstance, a threat that both astonished and quietened him, and I left the house without interruption.

On the next day we continued our march on the frozen river and stopped in another small village at night and the next day. There was nothing in particular happened this day except a wrestling match between McDonell and a young Russian peasant in which McDonell got a heavy fall to the vexation of Donohue, who shouted to McDonell to knock the Russian down; but McDonell did not think proper to obey him and I was glad he did not, for he got his fall fairly and had he struck the peasant it would doubtless have caused a row.

We were now within 28 versts of Voronesh, the end of our long march, and we were impatient to reach the place.

Voronesh, on the right bank of the River Voronesh, a tribulary of the Don, had been established in 1586 as a frontier fort against the Tartars. In 1694 Peter the Great had started a shipbuilding industry there. In 1803 a University was founded and, during the Crimean War, the town was the principal centre for allied prisoners of war. It is impossible to say how many prisoners there were at Voronesh, but no more than ninety returned. Allowing for deserters, who generally did not return, and the relatively small numbers of allied soldiers actually taken by the Russians, it is doubtful if the total number imprisoned there was more than 200.

The town is the capital of the region named after it, and is about 550 miles from Sebastopol. It had taken George Newman three months to get there.

During the last ('39–'45) war it was the farthest east that the German Army penetrated into Russia.

CHAPTER SEVEN

Bleak Winter
February – April

VORONESH

I liked the appearance of the town as we went in.

We started early the next morning and continued our journey on the river for some time and then turned off it. The weather was intensely cold, and Donohoe and Chapman put on their forage caps as they entered the town on purpose to cut a dash, and they got their ears frost bitten in consequence. I liked the appearance of the town as we went in. I saw there was plenty of pigeons and jackdaws, like the last town we were in. We passed through the market place and had a mob of spectators attracted chiefly, I believe, by the dragoons' red cloaks and blue forage caps with yellow bands.

We were drove into the yard of a large prison (for we all rode into the town) and, at the gates, there stood the chief part of my old comrades. There was great hand-shaking and many enquiries as to how we fared on the road. Jack-of-Clubs shook hands with me for full ten minutes and wanted to kiss me, but I would not stand that. I was invited by all hands to have dinner with them, but could only dine with one party.

I learnt that on their arrival in this town they had been placed in the prison until a large house in the town had been fitted up for their reception, and they expected to move into it on this very evening. Although they were stopping in a prison, they had full liberty to go where they liked in the town.

Their pay was still the same, and each man bought and ate whatever best suited his palate. They also told us that the party that preceded us on the road were in a house in the town, but were coming to the fresh house when it was ready; and that there was a sergeant major of the 44th regiment among them and that all hands disliked him.

After I had dined, a sergeant came and marched the five of us, Way, McDonell, Donohoe, Chapman and me down to the police master. We were shewn into a kind of office and requested to take off our caps. After a short stay the police master came in and enquired if any of us could speak Dutch. He was a very fat, jolly man and brought a decanter and glasses and gave each a glass of good Walki. Our names were then put down and we were told our numbers on the list. After this we were marched back to the prison and told to fetch our bundles. We were then marched to another office, where all they did was to stare us out of countenance and then let us go. I think now they were studying our features in case we should attempt to escape.

When we left this place we were marched to the new reception house and left there. Thus, though we were the last party to arrive, we were the first into permanent dwelling. We found several carpenters at work upstairs fitting up very rough kinds of beds round the walls of the different rooms. They consisted of rough boards placed upon the forms, or long stools cut in lengths to fit from one wall to the other, so that there was one large bed extending all round the room. The boards were covered with straw and a very large coarse kind of canvas, spread and nailed all over it. There was no bedding of any description, but there were some rough-made tables and forms in each room.

The rooms were generally large. Some of them were very large and opened one into another by folding doors; but the patent bedsteads prevented them from being opened. The windows were large and double-framed, as most windows in Russia are in consequence of the intense cold in the winter.

The house was very large and had been a handsome residence. There was a large balcony in front supported by four strong columns and guarded by a high railing, the entrance to which was through a double pair of glass doors. There was plenty of ovens to heat the rooms, and in a large yard there was some stabling and a cookhouse with a large oven for cooking in. There was two flights of stairs: one at each end of the house, one leading to the yard only and the other to the yard and street. There was a large pair of folding gates to the yard, that opened to the street.

Donohoe had a comrade of the name of Driscoll, a man of his own regiment and taller than himself, who had been taken prisoner with him and Chapman and had come on by himself after those two had gone into hospital. He had some money of Donohoe's and now invited him and Chapman and McDonell to have some dinner with him. Donohoe wanted me to go with them but I declined.

884 Private Denis Driscoll had enlisted on the 6th June 1846. He was 27 at the time of the Crimean War, and was finally discharged as unfit on the 4th August 1864.

The old sailor soon after went out to buy provisions for himself, as it appeared that our mess was to be broken up. When he was gone I was left by myself and walked up and down the rooms to pass away the time. While I was walking the sergeant major of the 44th Regiment came in with two respectable men to inspect the place. He passed within two feet of me and as I had my old regimental coat on, could not help seeing that I was an English sergeant. I fully expected he would speak but, although he passed so near me, he did not even give me a word or nod. This struck me that the men had not spoken ill of him without reason. He passed me again on the way out, but in the same contemptible manner.

Just as it was getting dark, the whole of the party from the prison came in and, as the rooms upstairs were not completed, they occupied the lower ones for the night, plenty of straw being given to lie upon and fire lit in the ovens to warm the place. I joined the party of the sailors in a game of four handed cribbage and we played some time, we were interrupted by the entrance of the sergeant major (whose name I found was O'Neale) with his face covered with blood from a wound at the corner of his mouth.

There was a little army of Russians with him (or rather, police, but they all dress alike, and it was long before I knew the difference). He asked for and looked about for Donohoe but Donohoe was nowhere to be found with us. O'Neale told us that Donohoe had struck him and if he could find him he would have him locked up. He met with no sympathy from any of the party, many of whom told him that it served him right and wished him some more.

It appeared that the party of which Donohoe formed part, when they left me, went to an eating house and dined and afterwards they went to a Walki shop and drank freely. Driscoll then took the whole party to his place (increased by a young fellow of the 7th Regiment, named and titled Corporal Walsh). There was a tea urn in their dwelling, lent by some gentleman for the use of the whole. Driscoll invited the others to have some tea and went to the urn; but O'Neale would not let him have it although it was idle, telling him he had no right to it. High words ensued; Donohoe gave O'Neale a topper that cut his mouth.

When O'Neale and the police left us they went to a Walki shop and there found Donohoe and Co. The police proceeded to make a prisoner of Donohoe, but found they had caught a tartar, for he secured an old stool and in a moment broke it and retained one of the legs. The lights were blown out and a battle royal commenced. The party fought their way backwards down a court in the direction of the police officer, where there was a sentry with a brass helmet and a brass battle axe guarding the entrance. The sentry caught hold of Donohoe, who soon got the battle axe from him and laid him on the floor with a blow of his own weapon; but the space being much wider they got round the whole party and, in spite of

Mr. Donohoe's exertions with the battle axe, they took the whole party prisoners, except Driscoll and Chapman, who managed to escape.

The next morning O'Neale came in about 8 o'clock, and a person with him, who we were told was the police officer put in charge of us by the police master. There was also an interpreter and, through him, we were informed that the sergeant major was put in command of us all under the police master; and that the non-commissioned officers among the prisoners were to consider themselves under his authority and enable him to keep order and discipline among the whole of the prisoners; and wound up by ordering all hands to remain in the house and not to leave it without his permission.

A great deal of grumbling and cursing took place at such an order, for hitherto they had not been under the least restraint and could roam about the town when and as long as they thought proper. The sailors were the first to dispute O'Neale's authority—saying that they would not mind being under the command of a soldier, providing he was a good one and had been fairly taken, but they would not obey a man who all believed to be a deserter, and that, if they must be under authority, they had their own boatswain and carpenter, their petty officers, and they would be answerable to them or any Russian the police master thought proper to put over them, but not O'Neale. This caused a discussion and ended by the boatswain and carpenter being put in charge of the sailors.

Many of the soldiers now spoke up, asking O'Neale who he thought would obey him when they all had such good reason to think he was a deserter. The whole discussion closed with groans, whistles, hisses and many, to shew their independence, walked out of the house for no other purpose than to let O'Neale see that they set his assumed authority at naught.

During the day I received a note from Donohoe, asking me to bring them something to eat, and their cloaks and sheepskins. I took them what they sent for and a rouble besides from his comrade Driscoll. I found them locked in a middling sized room with two windows heavily barred. There were several Russian prisoners in the same place and three or four women. The guard obliged them by bringing them as much Walki as they required, for which favour the guard took care to charge about treble the price they paid for it. They had some packs of cards and altogether were making themselves remarkably comfortable under the circumstances.

We moved this day from the lower rooms into the upper ones. The sailors got two rooms to themselves and I took up my position in the front centre room leading on to the balcony. I had no comrade and was far from being comfortable. I did not like the company of the men who stopped in my room, and I determined to leave it as soon as possible. In the next room to me there was a trumpet major of the 4th Light Dragoons, taken at Balaclava. He was a Scotsman and by name Hugh Crawford. He was a good musician, and a gentleman in the town had lent him an eight-keyed flute and he often enlightened us with his music. We soon became very intimate, and I always found him a good fellow.

Private Wightman of the 17th Lancers, describing the Charge wrote:

"I then rode towards Private Samuel Parkes of the 4th Light Dragoons, who, supporting with one arm the wounded Trumpet Major Crawford of his regiment was, with the other, cutting and slashing at the enemy surrounding him. I struck in to aid the gallant fellow, who was not overpowered until his sword was shot away, when he and the Trumpet Major where taken prisoner."

Private Parkes of the 4th Light Dragoons was awarded

the Victoria Cross for his part in the Charge of the Light Cavalry. He was Lord George Paget's servant. Lord George commanded the 4th at the Charge and is well known as having smoked a cigar during the action. In fact, Parkes had to remind him to draw his sword, which he did as they entered the Russian battery together.

This evening we had a visitor in the shape of a servant girl with no nose. She came in with a small accordion in her hand and soon began making a noise which was anything but harmonious or pleasing with the instrument, and dancing from one room to another through the passage, up and down the stairs as though she were bewitched. She continued these capers three or four nights, but at last discontinued her visits.

On the following night I was talking to Way (the old sailor who had come up with me) and I told him in the course of conversation how uncomfortable I was, and he invited me to come into his room with the sailors and mess with them, to which I consented. I took what things I had and shifted my quarters as quickly as possible. The same day O'Neale came round with a paper and pencil and said that he knew a gentleman who had promised to give him some shirts and stockings. I did not ask him to put my name down although I wanted a shirt badly, for I did not like him since the time he had passed me so disdainfully. He asked every other person in the room personally whether they wanted such things, but he passed me by, thus convincing me that he had no favourable opinion of me, as I believe, because I befriended Donohoe. He left the room but returned in about half an hour and called me out of the room by my name; and I don't know how he came to know my name, but when I went out to him he demanded to know who had given me liberty to leave the room and ordered me to go back to it, which I refused to do. He told me he would report me to the police master and I told him he might go and hang himself. We got to high words, but I was determined to stop where I was as long as the sailors were agreeable to my doing so.

O'Neale and two sergeants of the cavalry, one belonging to the 13th Light Dragoons and the other to the 17th Lancers, had a little room to themselves, which was comfortably furnished and had a little fire grate in it. It was a very comfortable quarter and they took good care to keep it to themselves, so in the dispute I asked him, if he so particularly wanted a sergeant to stop in the room I had vacated, why he did not send one of his companions, adding that they were both senior sergeants to me and, by the rules of the service, should be the first for duty.

"But", I continued, "both you and they have taken care to make yourselves comfortable and now find fault with me for attempting to do the same for myself. What, are they better than me?", I asked. "I consider myself the best sergeant in the house and have done more for my country than all of you put together, and can say with a clear conscience that I was taken prisoner in fair fight and with no fault of my own, and I doubt if all three of you can say the same."

He got very vexed at this, but I found that I was too good a lawyer for him and he left me. I mention this affair as it explains the bad manner in which I was ever after treated by O'Neale.

Donohoe and the others were released this evening with a severe reprimand from the police master, and they got drunk again to shew their gratitude.

I spoke to Crawford this night about the shirts that were to be given out, and he told me that it was not only shirts but many other things that were to be distributed among us, but we should have to wait some little time before we got them. He then went on to tell me that there was a Scots gentleman in the town of the name of Macpherson, holding a situation under the Russian Government of teacher of foreign languages at a large cadet school in the town, and that he was a great friend of the English prisoners, that he (Crawford), O'Neale and the two cavalry sergeants went, one each day in turns, to dine with him and spend the evening with him. Macpherson, pitying the destitute condition of many of the men, had written to several parts of the country where there was English residents, and various collections had been made to provide us with some kind of clothing; and part of the money had already been transmitted to Macpherson, and more would be coming shortly; that he, Macpherson, not liking to be seen too deeply interested in it (through holding his situation from the Russian Government) had commissioned Sergeant Major O'Neale and the cavalry sergeants to get the men's names and what they required and where to buy and distribute the things, but Macpherson would come occasionally to see that each man was properly provided for.

On the next day I went to O'Neale and asked him to put my name down for two shirts and pairs of stockings. He demurred about doing it, and I had to inform him that if he did not do it I should make application to Macpherson myself; upon which he put my name down, but it was some time before any of us got them.

We had women come to visit us to apply for our washing, and the men in our room selected a respectable-looking woman to wash for them. She charged 2 copecks for each piece, unless it was the sailors' thick, large blue flannel shirts, for which she charged one copeck extra, and used to wash them well.

My comrade and I pulled along together very comfortably. I was always employed as market man, because I could speak more Russian than Way. I used generally to start for the market before breakfast, for the market is open very early, and after breakfast time pretty well empty of eatables. When I returned with what I had bought, Way would prepare the dinner and after I had had my breakfast I would look to the cooking of it. When it was cooked I would bring it up and we would both set to. After we had done Way would wash up and put away the remnants for tea and supper.

We had an old man attend our dwelling five or six times a day, with a large brass kettle with a fire in the centre of it, like a tea urn. He sold what he was pleased to call 'tea', which consisted of hot water made very sweet with a bad kind of honey, very common in Russia, and supplying the place of moist sugar. He generally carried a bottle of milk under his arm and used to charge a copeck for a small tumbler of his apology for tea, with a small drop of milk in it. He got plenty of custom during the cold weather, and when summer commenced he dropped the tea and began a kind of beer made from herbs, and sometimes he would tempt us with ice cream. The old fellow was indispensable to me morning and evening, for with a couple of glasses of his hot stuff and some bread and butter I used to make a tolerable meal.

During the cold weather we lived almost entirely on beef, which we brought in a frozen condition. So hard was it that it was considered a bit of hard work to cut it up for use. We could get the best joints at 3 copecks per pound, but suet and fat were scarce. We used to thicken our soup with a kind of grain called (in England) millet, which we found a good thing for the dysentery. Bread was good and cheap: a loaf weighing about 3 pounds would cost 3 copecks. Potatoes were very cheap and we could get about half a bushel for six copecks, about $2\frac{1}{2}$d English.

I remember that I went to the cookhouse as usual to look after the cooking, when I found the old serf, whose duty it was to bring boiling water and light the fire, very busy in pulling the pots out of the oven. I entered just in time to see him upset mine, and all its valuable contents rolling in the wood ashes in the oven. I ran at the old fellow and tried to get the hook with which the pots are put into and taken out of the oven, for the purpose of securing anything that might remain in the bottom of the pot, but the old fellow appeared to think I wanted it for a more sinister purpose and, instead of giving it he struck me on the head with it. Losing my dinner was bad enough, but to have a topple into the bargain was more than a philosopher could bear, so the old fellow soon found himself minus his weapon and himself on the broad of the back on the floor.

Just in the middle of the shindy the police officer in charge of us came in and, seeing his domestic in such a position and I standing over him, he made a rush at me and aimed a blow at me with a good lump of a walking cane, but I drew back and avoided the blow and made a suitable return for his intended civility. He was astonished at my temerity and did not offer to renew the attack, and I gave him to understand that if Nicholas was to strike me I would return the compliment, and I marched out of the room in triumph.

He—the police officer—never forgave me and I several times caught him pointing me out to other people, once the police master, and once to Mr. Macpherson; no doubt representing me as a very turbulent character, for he would pantomime the scene to a nicety.

On another occasion I attempted to warm some milk for my breakfast in one of the ovens that heated our room; and I believe there had been an order given that we were not to cook in those places, but I never heard it. I left my pot in the oven for a few minutes, and when I returned I found my milk spilt upon the floor of the passage and the serf, who had charge of the house, busily engaged in breaking my pot. Of course I expostulated, but the only answer I got was a piece of the broken utensil thrown at my head and followed up by a furious attack with a piece of firewood.

I never came across such a people for striking as the Russians, especially if they hold any kind of office. Of course I was not going to put up with such treatment from him, when I would not allow his master to do the same. I therefore gave the Jack-in-office a walloping and, my steam being properly up when I got him on the floor, I tried to ram his head into the oven, and I have no doubt I should have succeeded only for the interference of some of my fellow prisoners. This job was soon reported to the police officer and I was set down as one of the most refractory of the English.

We had no regular hours for meals: each man ate when he thought fit. In our room the men messed together by twos and threes, except one party of six. There was but the one oven for cooking in and the hour for dinner would be whenever it was ready. Thus we were eating the whole day through.

The sailors strove to keep their room clean and decent, and for this purpose we would take it in turns, by twos, to get up in the morning and holystone the tables and forms and wash out the room and keep it clean and tidy through the day, and supply drinking water. There was one other soldier (a man of my own regiment) in the room, but he did not like the cleaning job and got turned out, after which they would not allow any other soldier but me to stop in the room with them.

As a general rule I passed the day as follows: rise about 7 a.m., strip and have a good hunt for 'hayseeds with legs on them' shave and wash, go to market. Breakfast, take down the dinner, return and play cards or read until ready, running down to the cookhouse several times during the process of cooking to see that all was right (for sometimes the other men would pull any other pots out of the oven to get their own in, which generally ended in a fight if caught in the act). Dinner, sleep, read, play cards, tea, cards or skylarking or singing—generally cards—until 11 o'clock p.m. Make my bed with what clothes I had and lie down and listen to the sailors' yarns until I fell asleep.

There was some good cribbage players among the sailors, and we often used to make four, at a copeck per corner per game. The old carpenter, who was called Chippy, was always ready to play and many a time he has tried to beat me, but in vain, although generally he won when playing with any other person. The sailors were a good set of fellows and I was as comfortable as I could be under the circumstances.

In the course of about three weeks O'Neale began distributing the clothing and, though he knew I was nearly naked he served all the rest first, even men who had come in since me. I was much provoked at such pitiful spite and determined to ask Mr. Macpherson myself as soon as I could, and a circumstance happened shortly that brought him to our place.

The circumstance was as follows: shortly after his release from prison, Donohoe, McDonell and others who we could not find out, in a drunken freak, insulted a lady and afterwards an officer. There was a great row about it, and the police master came up to our house and, through an interpreter, told us that if we did not put a stop to such proceedings he would be obliged to stop our liberty and pay and put us in close confinement and on Russian convict diet (black break and white water). He advised us to find the guilty party and punish them ourselves, saying that he did not want to bring us to be punished as the Russians were.

When he was gone, there was a general assembly of all the prisoners, and three of the oldest soldiers and one of the eldest of the sailors formed themselves into a court martial, with power to order any number of lashes they might think proper in the circumstances, and also to call upon any person to inflict the punishment and upon any others to aid and assist.

The court, after a little deliberation, sentenced the two culprits to two dozen lashes each, on the seat of honour, and called upon Trumpet Major Crawford to inflict the punishment, and several others to aid and assist. The punishment was administered with a heavy belt and the trumpet major done his duty and no mistake. The punishment must have been severe, by the writhing of the men.

That same evening Macpherson came and had us all assembled together. He told us of the danger of such doings, adding that the populace had risen against the Turks in another town, and had murdered about two hundred of them. He assured us that there was a great ill-feeling towards us in the town, and that it required but little to bring a mob about the house and serve us the same. He told us that there had been a report received detailing the particulars of the death of the soldier on the road, and the Governor of the town had assured him that others in the town knew of it besides himself, and, should they make it public, nothing would stop the people sacrificing the whole of us in revenge. He gave us much good advice as to our conduct and spoke in a kind, gentlemanly way.

After he had finished speaking I went to him and spoke for some clothing and told him how I had been delayed behind the others. He called O'Neale and told him to supply me with what I needed. He enquired how and why I was taken and praised the courage of the British at the battle of Inkerman, and said it was the greatest laurel England had ever won. He enquired if I had been ill, and on my telling him of the state of my stomach he said he would send me some medicine the next day that would cure it; and the next day he sent me a red liquid, of which I was to take two drops in a glass of water, six times a day, and I believe it cured me.

That same night some of our men went out and got drunk and kicked up a row in the town, and the upshot was that we had another court martial the next morning and another flogging match, and, if possible, they got it heavier and sharper than the first two. For some time after this flogging match the men bettered a little, but soon after began to fall off again.

On the second day after Macpherson's visit, O'Neale served me out with a piece of black cloth for trowsers and a piece of blue cloth for a jacket, a narrow piece of scarlet cloth to make the stripe for the trowsers. I was also measured for a pair of wellington boots. I also got a shirt and a pair of socks; but O'Neale stinted me (and I think purposely) in the black cloth for, when I took it to one of our tailors (of whom we had several) to suit them out for me, he couldn't make it enough, try which way he would, and at last I was obliged to get another piece and patch to complete them. The whole of the tailors were most busily engaged and I could not persuade any of them to work for me until they had finished what they had got. As I was in a hurry to get my trowsers done I determined to try and make them myself. So I set to work, and a pretty good job I had of it. I had never tackled tailoring on so large a scale before and I was a full fortnight before I had completed my job, and I don't think I should ever have finished if only for the advice of the sailors, combined with a little of their assistance. I saved up 60 copecks, with which I bought lining and lined them, for the cloth was precious thin. I also saved 80 copecks, with which I bought a kind of cloak from one of the prisoners. It was of a very coarse, rough, black cloth and had been issued to the man by the Russian Government, and many others had cloaks like it. I got it cut up into a shape to make a surtout. I got a Russian tailor in the town up in my room, and by general perseverance I made him understand how I wanted it put together and then gave it to him to finish; and I had to be very careful in saving to pay for it. I also cut up my old coattee and turned it and made a kind of undress jacket from it; but it was a world of trouble, and Robinson Crusoe was a fool to me for patience and contriving.

The sailors who needed it were served out with blue cloth,

enough to make a trowsers and jacket, and each had a pair of boots. They made their own trowsers and done them well; but the short round jackets was too much for them and they were sent to a Dutch tailors in the town with an English one for a pattern, but they made an awful job of it, to the great consternation of the sailors.

The cavalrymen were served with enough cloth to make a stable jacket and trousers and cap, but the cavalry had a great advantage over the infantry in the superior making of their clothing. They turned their regimental coats and made good jackets of them and the cloth that was issued to them served to make them two pairs of trowsers. I cannot understand why a cavalryman should be so much better clad than an infantry-man. I cannot but see that an infantryman requires good, substantial cloth for marching through a bush or building batteries or digging trenches. It strikes me that on a campaign the infantry had much the harder work of the two and are much the worse clothed . . . but to proceed.

Each man had provided himself with trimming for his clothing and each had some peculiar whim of his own to satisfy, so we had many kinds of dress among us.

On every Sunday we were recruited by fresh arrivals and my little comrade Farquharson the trumpeter joined us, all right again; and one Sunday we had a man of 33rd Regiment arrive with a crutch and another (a nice looking young fellow named Lucas) of the 4th Light Dragoons, deficient of one arm, which he lost at Balaclava by a sabre cut. We also had a great many deserters arrive and, before it was found they were deserters, many of them got served out with clothing; but afterwards they were more particular as to who they gave it to.

Farquharson says that many of the deserters tried to join the Russian forces, but were told that if they could not serve in the British army they could not be trusted in the Russian.

The police officer began to be very uncertain in the discharge of his duties, especially in the important matter of pay. Sometimes we actually had to wait ten and twelve days for our money and, at last, we went to the police master and made a report at his negligence, which so vexed the police master that he took all manner of means of annoying us. He attempted first to confine us to barracks but, failing in this, would come poking about the rooms at 10 o'clock at night and count the men in the rooms to find if any were out.

He would then march up to the table and blow the candle out and order us to lie down. He discharged the old serf who brought us water and many times were we left without any in consequence, and when our firewood ran short he would not trouble himself to get more and we were many times without firing. Besides which he would look about for drunken men and as sure as he found any he would have an escort of police and send them to the lock-up. Also if he found any men out of their rooms when he came round at night he would place an escort at the front door and apprehend them as they came in and send them off to the lock-up; and to degrade them as much as possible, he would send them sweeping the streets for two or three days at a time, keeping them during that time in the lock-up.

Of course he was much disliked and many threats were made to serve him out but none put into force. This game was carried on for some weeks, and, one night as we were going to bed, one of the sailors left the room for some purpose and we determined to have a game with him and we filled a quart cup with water and placed it on top of the door on a balance, leaving the door ajar so that when the absentee should open the door to come in the cup and water should fall on him. To make certain of the fall of the tin cup, two of the men provided themselves with dish cloths which, when the door began to move, they were to throw at the door, so that it would be sure to overbalance the cup and cause it to fall.

We waited a long time for the return of the sailor. At length we heard footsteps approaching and presently after the door began to move slowly open. The two dishcloths were thrown together and done their work effectively, but guess our astonishment when we saw the police officer bounce into the room in a great rage, saturated with water, instead of the absent sailor. The occurrence and his appearance were so extremely ridiculous that we could not refrain from a hearty laugh, which put Mr. Officer in a worse pet than ever. After some time we tried to explain to the officer that the cup of water was not intended for him but for one of the sailors, and mentioned the name; but Mr. Officer got an opinion into his head that the absent sailor had put the cup there, and declared he would send him to the lockup and flog him. In vain we tried to explain that the fault was ours and not the man's. He waited a long time but the sailor did not return and, at last, he went away and we thought the affair was dropped; but early next morning he came with some soldiers and marched the sailor off. We all determined to go to the police master and make a complaint of the conduct of the officer, and many of the soldiers and one of the cavalry sergeants joined us and, after cleaning ourselves, we started in a body.

We were not all admitted into the office, but only a few of us and I, as sergeant, was one of the number; but I must relate a scene that took place while we were there. There was a civilian in the office guarded on both sides by a policeman. It appeared that the man had entered into a contract to take provisions to the army in the Crimea in his old waggon, and with two horses. He had received a sum of money in advance to support himself and cattle on the road, but the old chap had gone on the spree and spent the money and carried it so far that he had sold one of his horses and could not, in consequence, fulfil his engagement and was now a prisoner through default.

After waiting some time the police master made his appearance wrapped in a dressing gown. He bowed to us as he entered and began to examine the civilian before listening to our complaint. The police stated the circumstance of the case, and the police master folded his arms on his breast and asked for his (the culprit's) defence. I could understand but little of what he said in extenuation of his conduct, for he cried so much and spoke in such a singing manner that much better Russians than me might have been puzzled to understand him. When he had finished, the police master gave a peculiar grin and began to roll up the sleeves of his dressing gown above his elbows, doing it very slowly as though he was afraid of distressing himself. He then ordered him to kneel down and taking hold of his chin he put his face looking upwards to himself. He then commenced squaring away at the face in a manner that would have done honour to Bendigo or Ben Caunt or any of the Prize Ring. I thought he did not intend to strike him but was shortly undeceived, for he set to right and left on the countenance that was kept uplifted towards him by the two police.

William Thompson, alias Bendigo, and Ben Caunt were well-known prize fighters. Thompson was born in 1811 and died, a Methodist minister, in 1888. Caunt died in 1861. They were opponents on three occasions: in 1835, 1838 when Caunt beat Bendigo in the 75th round after a riot, and in 1845 when Bendigo got his revenge.

I had said before that the police master was a very fat person with a great rotundity of paunch. He continued his violent exercise so long that the perspiration ran down his fat cheeks with the exertion, nor did he leave off until he was fairly exhausted. The culprit was then taken away to the outer room where, by his cries, we could tell that the policemen were giving him something of the same sort.

This Police Master, whose name was Ikienioff, was not averse to punishing the English prisoners in this way, as Farquharson knew to his cost. Describing this man as "a burly man, some six feet in height and 15 or 16 stone in weight. He came up to me and pushed me on the breast with his hand, saying 'Is that English?' I said nothing and he gave me a harder push, repeating the question. Then, before I knew, he gave me a tremendous blow with his fist on the right side of the head—at the same time opening up on me a volley of abuse in Russian." He and the sergeant of police so nearly killed the poor trumpeter that, on a complaint being made, they were both sent to the Crimea.

The police master, after he had taken time to regain his breath, turned to know our business, which was soon told and, just as we finished, in came our officer himself. He was in a great hurry and very much frightened, for he had but just learnt the movement we had made against him. He stammered out some apologies to the police master and said he had already released the prisoner. The police master gave him a great blowing up and told us he would send us another officer in his place; and then he made a long oration on the very bad conduct of the English and made many threats as to how he would serve us if we did not reform. We tried to explain that the fault only lay in a few, and we asked him to take those away from the rest, and keep them in confinement by themselves. He promised to do so but did not keep his promise.

After this we found ourselves a little more comfortable,

and the officer we got in place of the first one did not trouble us much but was generally behind in his payment, a fact that I think originated with the higher authority, for he often assured us he could not obtain the money to pay us with.

One day Donohoe got very drunk and, as usual, kicked up a row. He fought with a man in his own room and in the conflict got a severe fall that hurt him inside. He still kept in his room and drank Walki as a medicine for several days but, getting worse, he was obliged to get to hospital.

Our numbers now were getting strong through so many new arrivals. I observed that those who came last were in general the worst behaved. One day one of them stole a piece of cloth from another man that had been given to him to make a jacket. We had another general assembly and court martial and he received the same punishment as the former ones.

About this time I had managed to save money enough to get my jacket made and I had it trimmed with a good imitation of silver lace and, when it was finished and I had got a blue cloth forage cap made with an imitation silver lace band and buttons, I cut a great dash through the streets of the town, and the Russian soldiers, whom I would often meet in my rambles, would stop and stand at attention with their caps in their hand until I had passed. In this manner they always salute their officers and I took care to return the compliment as gentlemanly as possible. This was no rare occurrence, but as often as I showed my figure in the street, and I really think that if I had stopped there much longer I should have fancied myself an officer.

One day a respectable-looking civilian came into our room and asked for the carpenter. He spoke French and I was brought forward as interpreter. He wanted the carpenter to build him a boat and he would pay him well for it, but old Chippy declared that as he was a prisoner he would be one and not set to work to learn the enemy how to build boats.

The civilian was eager to get him to work and called several times, but Chippy remained obdurate and would not work for him.

I must now say a word about the interpreter. He was a Welshman and had come to the country with his wife some years before the war commenced as a working engineer or millwright. He had got on well at first but, partly through misfortune and partly through drink, had brought poverty on himself. His wife was also Welsh and had once been in good circumstances, which could soon be learnt by her conversation. The man was small and thin but his wife was much taller and much stouter than he, and they had one child, a boy. Thompson, for such was his name, and his wife, were very handy to us in interpreting for us, and he would come every day to go with any sick to the hospital, where his services were, to the sick, invaluable, in describing their diseases to the doctors. He was always sent for when anything went wrong and, though the men in general considered him lazy, drunken and lying, yet I don't know what we should have done without him.

One day the Trumpet Major Crawford came in and told us that Mrs. Thompson and the child were actually starving through want, and he proposed that we had a collection for their relief, which was agreed to on the condition that the money collected should be given to the woman herself, as everyone thought that if Thompson got it he would get drunk with it. The collection was made and I forget how much was collected, and was gratefully received by the woman. The practice continued during our stay in the town. On each pay day, and we were always paid five days' money at once, or sometimes ten, for in the first instance each man got a rouble for himself and in the latter he got two, which saved much trouble in getting change, a scarce article in this country. On each pay day, then, each man would give 3 copecks, or what he could afford, and which was always given to Mrs. Thompson.

There was another man, of the name of Wilson, in the town, who kept a sort of brazier's shop, selling and mending all kinds of tinware. He told us that he was an American, but I and many others did not believe him, for he could give no accurate account of that country. He often came to see us, and acted as interpreter for us, but very seldom. To judge by his appearance he was not doing very well in this country, though I never heard him complain.

There was also a Scotch lady, married to an old major in the Russian service, and Crawford was a great visitor there, being Scotch, and he used to tell me she often wished herself in her old country again. She was useful in letting us know the progress of the war and Russian opinion of it, and when anything extra was stirring she would let us know of it.

Macpherson provided the sick in hospital with tea and sugar, which I have said before was a great luxury in this country, and also used to pay one or two nurses to provide hot water for them and pay them greater attention than they were likely to get without it, and he would often visit them himself.

One morning about this time the whole house was thrown-into an uproar by Thompson bringing the news of the death of the Emperor Nicholas. We would scarcely believe it at first, for we knew Thompson to be a great liar; but other persons soon brought the news and, lastly, the church bells and the shutting of the shops confirmed the tidings. Our men were overjoyed at the tidings, for now there was some prospect of soon getting out of the country, and we made sure the war would soon be finished. All day long people were constrained to go to church to pray for the departed Emperor and swear allegiance to his successor. All the troops in the town were marched to church for the same purpose, and the police master was driving about the town like a mad thing, hunting everybody to church and closing the shops.

That evening there was great jollification in our house; every man was on the spree and merry songs and dances were the order of the evening, and many were the toasts wishing Old Nick a hot corner with his namesake.

Nicholas had died on the 18th February 1855. News of his death had reached the allies before Sebastopol on 6th March. He was succeeded by his eldest son, 37-year-old Alexander II.

CHAPTER EIGHT

Summer
April–August

ZOUAVES
From *The Illustrated London News*
2nd December 1854

The change from winter to summer was very sudden. A few days only elapsed and the trees that had so shortly before been glistening with frost were all in full leaf, and many of the early ones in full blossom, and we were glad to open our double windows and get a breath of cool air in our rooms; and the fleas appeared to spring spontaneously from the ground with the first warmth of the sun, and a miserable time we had of it.

Many of the sailors had been sent for by the police master to form a boat's crew. The ice on the river had broken up and hence the necessity for a boat as there was no bridge. Twelve of them agreed to go, and they were to have quarters close to the landing stage. They were to receive 40 copecks per day extra, which made their pay up to 60 copecks per day, an enormous rate of pay in Russia.

The boatswain had charge of the party. The boat pulled eight oars and the boatswain acted as coxswain, and a man-of-war's man as bowman. Two others were left in the house to cook and look after the things, but received the same pay as the rest and shared all perquisites. At the first, one of the 4th Light Dragoons went as cook but, being taken ill, had to leave, after which they put one of their own lads in his place.

The sailors took great pride in their job and kept their boat clean, and everything was conducted in Man-of-War style, and the boatswain bought an imitation gold lace band for his cap to make him look like an officer. The rest all turned out in blue frocks and trowsers and they made a very good-looking boat's crew, and many people came to see the English pull their boat. The boat was large and capable of holding a dozen people besides the crew. They had a plank to place on the shore for embarking and disembarking of passengers, which was kept very clean and, when any person entered the boat, a hand rail would be formed by one of the sailors holding one end of the boathook and another, in the boat, holding the other end. The remainder of the men would keep on the boat with the oars poised in the air and, when all the passengers were on board, the sailor who had been standing on shore would come on board, take in and stow away the plank and then take his seat and poise his oar in the air like the rest, while the bowman would shove her head round to the stream with the boat hook; and at the word of command 'Let Fall' every oar would drop in the water, and at the word 'Give Way' they would all bend together to the stroke, the boatswain steering.

No one but government people were allowed to enter the boat but the police master and governor and deputy governor of the town, with parties of ladies and gents, would often have a turn on the river in the boat, and the sailors used to earn a deal of money from these parties; and they scarcely ever rowed a government official across to the other side without being presented with a rouble, so that it was a very lucrative business.

There was a Walki shop close by the landing place and opposite the sailors' quarters, which took the most part of their earnings, and when they were all absent from the boat at once—which was often the case—the boatswain would collect them together by the sound from the call of his pipe, and the sailors, as soon as they heard the shrill command, would run to the boat like soldiers obeying the sound of the bugle.

This job lasted upwards of two months, until the water of the river, which had been much swollen by the thaw of the deep snow, had decreased so much as to enable the inhabitants to throw a temporary bridge over the stream.

These displays of nautical skill would have been in sharp contrast to the lack of it shewn by the Russian Navy of the period, which, when the Royal Navy appeared in the Black Sea, could think of nothing better to do than to scuttle itself at the entrance to Sebastopol harbour.

Madame Hommaire, when she was staying in Sebastopol in 1852, says that there it was currently and libellously reported that once, between Sebastopol and Odessa, the admiral was so utterly lost that the flag lieutenant, observing a village on shore, proposed to land and ask the way.

One night we retired to rest rather earlier than usual and had only just begun to doze, when the old serf came in bringing a little army of lighted candles on a tray with him, one of which he placed in each window with significant signs that we were not to blow them out. Just as the clocks struck twelve the whole of the church bells began to ring a merry peal. There are many churches in Voronesh and every Russian church had plenty bells and many of them very large and, as they were all at it together, you may be sure there was a pretty noise. The air vibrated with the din and the windows shook as though they would fall to pieces.

We wondered what it was all about, but soon found out that it was Easter Sunday morning. We looked from our windows and saw all the windows illuminated, similar to our own, and the churches and steeples; and in all the streets on both sides there are small stone posts in the kerb stones, the posts being about two feet high and five or six yards apart. On each of the posts there was placed a lamp similar to what our showmen burn on the stage of their travelling theatres. It is a kind of iron, with a large wick of cotton in the centre and well supplied with grease. They looked remarkably well, especially in the long streets, but it was a queer kind of illumination to an Englishman.

The next morning, on going to market, I found the streets decorated with green boughs and the Russians kissing each other in the streets. I was much afraid that some of the female gender would salute me, but providence preserved me.

I met several processions of pictures and priests, with lighted tapers and swinging censers, parading the streets this day. In some processions there were ten or a dozen pictures of different sizes. Some were of Our Saviour, some of the Virgin Mary, and some had the Virgin with Our Redeemer as a child in her arms. Others were of different saints, but they were drawn and painted in such quaint dress that I could not make them out. I remember seeing one who must have been a modern saint, for he was drawn in a kind of cut-away green coat and a large pair of black boots that reached the knees, and he had wings at his back. I saw that the people considered themselves highly honoured at being allowed to carry those pictures. I have seen well-dressed ladies carrying them through the street in the mud and dirt, and the people passing by would halt and cross themselves and drop on their knees to pray, and then would rush among the bearers to kiss the pictures. I have seen ladies get out of their carriages to kiss the pictures and many, not content with that, would go down on their hands and knees and crawl under them. These processions were very frequent after the fine weather commenced and the people were always quite as enthusiastic as on Easter Sunday.

I have since been told that, if our windows had not been illuminated on the commencement of the bells ringing, the populace would surely have broken them.

The exchanging of eggs was also an Easter custom and Madame Hommaire wrote at Easter 1838:

"A painter was brought expressly from Kherson to our entertainers' mansion for the purpose of painting more than 1,000 eggs, most of them adorned with cherubim, fat-cheeked angels, Virgins and all the saints in Paradise. Everyone was eager to assist in the preparation for merry-making, some put up swings, others arranged the ball-room, some were intent on their devotions, others half smothered themselves in the vapour baths. During all Easter week the peasant had the right to embrace whom-soever he pleased, not even excepting the Emperor and Empress. This is a relic of the old patriarchal manners which prevailed so long unaltered all over northern Europe."

One morning Thompson, our interpreter, came and told us that Donohoe had died during the night and was to be buried on the following day, and on the next morning we all cleaned ourselves and went to the hospital. Adjoining the dead house was a small chapel and the Russian priest asked if he should perform the funeral rites of the Russian church over our comrade. We gave our consent, and he was carried into the chapel and placed on a table in the centre of two other corpses, and we were encircled by a ring of lighted candles. The ceremony consisted chiefly of singing and waving the incense towards the different pictures of saints that were hung plentifully upon the walls of the chapel. After the ceremony was over we took the corpse to carry him to his grave, a distance of a mile and a half. We tried to carry him on our shoulders, but from the peculiar construction of the coffin could not manage it. We then got two pieces of stick and carried the coffin on them by our hands. The soldiers marched first in the rear of the corpse, two and two, and then about four yards apart and the sailors in the rear. We had many people to look at such a curious sight, but they would uncover and cross themselves as the corpse came near them.

When we had got some distance, the men who were carrying complained that they would surely let the corpse drop, as the road was very uneven and they could not help stumbling. We got an old peasant to lend us his vehicle. I forget whether it was a sleigh or waggon, but he carried the corpse as far as the church gates and then we carried it to the grave. A troop sergeant major of the cavalry produced a prayer book, and began the service for the dead at the church gates. We buried the poor fellow according to our church, although he had been buried, as our interpreter called it, by the Russian priest in the chapel.

There was a Roman Catholic chapel in the town, and many of our men who belonged to that persuasion attended it, but I never heard of a Protestant place of worship. There was some gentleman on this day at the funeral gave some money to be distributed among the men. I don't know how much, but it was distributed among the soldiers only, which gave great offence to the sailors, not for the value of the money but for the distinction it made.

One evening a cavalry sergeant came to me and asked if I had any objection to go to a house daily to teach a lady English, adding that he had attended there sometimes but had now a better place and was much occupied that he could not attend any longer. Of course I consented, and he told me to be ready to go with him the next morning and he would introduce me. Accordingly I got ready and went with him. On entering I saw a lady sitting on a sofa and talking to a gentleman. He was very small and pale and appeared to be in delicate health. There was two children—a boy about 4 years of age and a girl about 6 or 7. After the introduction my introducer left us and I found that the lady could speak English tolerably well and the gentleman, her brother, could also speak it pretty well, and the girl too, but the boy was not so forward.

I soon found out my duty, which was to attend every morning at 9 a.m. at which hour I always found the gentleman alone. The lady usually made her appearance at half past or a quarter before ten o'clock. Before her arrival her brother would get me to converse with him, and it was my duty to correct him if wrong in anything he said, or explain the meaning or proper pronunciation of any word he might require. When the lady came we would all adjourn for breakfast, where I got some good coffee, a rare treat for me. After breakfast her brother would leave to attend to his business, for he was an attorney, so the lady told me. After his departure, the children would bring their books and I would hear them read and catechise them for a short time, and afterwards I would hear the lady herself, correcting her when wrong, and generally ended in a long conversation on the different customs of our countries.

She had learnt French and German from books and had made good progress in English from the same source, but owned that she found English the most difficult. She told me her husband was a colonel in the Gendarmerie in St. Peterburg and that she was stopping with her brother for the benefit of her health.

The first morning I remained with her until 12 o'clock, and when I rose to take my leave she gave me half a rouble for my trouble, asking if I were satisfied. I replied in the affirmative, and she added that she preferred paying daily, and so did I. So we were agreed on that important point.

After that me and my pupil got along very comfortably, but the lady would often put very puzzling questions to me. One day in our conversation she asked me the meaning of the word *fast*. I answered, "to be quick, or sharp". She brought down an English dictionary and found it correct. Then she brought an English novel and opened it and shewed me a paragraph of a lover making his horse *fast* to a tree, and wanted to know how a horse could be quick if it were tied up. I tried to explain that anything tied up or locked up was *made fast*, but she was not satisfied and said the English had many words that meant two separate things.

Another day she wanted to know why we called military vessels "Men-of-War" and yet, speaking of any one of them, we called it "she". I had one answer for her troublesome questions, and there were many, which was that it was the custom of our country, which puzzled her as much as she did me. One morning, as soon as I entered she came with a book in her hand and she said she was glad I had come for after I had left the day previous she had met with a word in that book that she could not find the meaning of. She had searched the dictionary, she said, but there was no such word in it. I was eager myself to see a word that was not in the dictionary, and she opened the book. It was *Jacob Faithful*, and the word was *Lobscouse*. I had hard matter to refrain from a fit of laughter, but I made her understand that *Lobscouse* was just a word that sailors used for their hard meat stewed with vegetables and ship's biscuit, and she declared she would have some made, which she did and said, next day, that she did not like it.

On one Saturday, when I was taking my leave, she invited me to come to dinner on the Sunday. I thanked her and promised to come, and next day down I went. I was surprised on entering to find six other ladies besides herself in the room. She welcomed me kindly, but I did not half like my position, the only male among seven ladies and six of them entire strangers and evidently myself a curiosity by the manner in which they regarded me and whispered to each other. I withstood this powerful battery of bright eyes for some time, but mortal flesh could not hold out against so many, so I rose and made my excuse to my pupil that some English gentleman was coming from Moscow to visit us and I wished to be present. I was glad to make my escape and breathed much freer when I got outside.

The next morning, as soon as I went down, she commented about my going away, and asked if I did not like her company. Of course I answered that I was always happy in such respectable company.

"But you were not happy," says she "you were, what is the

word? "Here she stopped and fetched the dictionary and, soon after, found what she wanted.

"You were very shy—ashamed—and ran away."

I could feel the blood rush to my face and I must have cut a queer figure. She enjoyed my confusion very much, but invited me to come on the next Sunday and, as I could not think of an excuse, I was compelled to accept it.

There was but two of the fair sex there that day, and her brother was there also, so I got on better than the first time. One morning her brother brought me a map of Sebastopol, shewing all the British and French batteries with the number of guns in each, the position of every regiment, both English and French and Turks, and he asked me to point out the place where I was taken, which I could easily do. He then brought me a similar map of Balaclava, which not only showed the different batteries and the number of guns but even shewed the trench work thrown up for its defence and the whole of the cavalry regiments.

On another morning he translated to me from a Russian newspaper the account of the attack upon Kertch, telling me that the English had run their bayonets into women and children.

The town of Kertch lies at the entrance of, and is the key to, the Sea of Azov. On the 25th May 1855 a combined British, Turkish and French expedition, under General Sir George Brown, landed and soon captured the port. Turning northwards the troops marched to Yeni Kale, destroying Russian shipping as they went. The Royal Navy entered the Sea of Azov and successfully took control of it.

By mid-June the expedition was, however, recalled, leaving the Turkish contingent, 1,000 British and 1,000 French troops as garrison.

Whilst it is not true to say that the troops had run their bayonets into women and children, the episode was certainly marred by some cruelty to the civil population.

I found the lady as credulous and superstitious as the peasantry, for, one day she told me a tale about a Bishop of Voronesh, who, while he lived, was a very pious and charitable man; that he died upwards of two hundred years ago and that, while workmen were at work digging the foundations of a church, they came upon his body. This, she said, was not long ago, so that doubtless the bishop had been in the ground for two hundred years. When found, his body was not in the least decayed but as fresh as when he had died; that a silver coffin had been made for the body and that it had a glass top so that the corpse could be seen; that the corpse had the power of working miracles and had cured many diseases by being touched; and that people made pilgrimages from all parts of Russia to pray to him, and that she herself worshipped him.

One day I asked her if she did not read the Bible and why she did not let the children read it. She replied that the Bible was not a fit book for women and children to read, that there were many indelicate things in it not fitting to be read. I tried to make her understand the difference, but she said what was fit to be read she heard read in church by the priests. On another day we had an argument whether it was right to pray to the Virgin Mary, she contending that it was especially right for mothers to pray to Her, as She had been a mother Herself and knew the pains of childbirth by experience and could therefore sympathise with a mother more than a deity.

We often had arguments on this and other religious subjects, but I could not argue her out of her beliefs.

Once we were talking of the working classes of England, and I told her that a person was considered poor indeed who could not afford to have their tea morning and evening, and that most working classes had feather beds to lie on with plenty of clothes and carpets on their floors and sofas in their rooms. She was greatly astonished and did not appear to believe me.

One day I went down to her house and, on entering, found a tall soldier-like, good-looking man talking with her brother. Her brother introduced the gentleman as the lady's husband come from St. Petersburg. After some little talk I was informed by the brother that the lady was ill, and that he would send for me as soon as she got better and able to go on with her lessons.

I never saw her after for after waiting some time, I ventured to call one morning and her brother informed me that she was no better and had been ordered by the doctor to live in the cow-shed with the cows, from which I concluded that she was suffering from consumption. I called several times afterwards with the same success.

One day we had three English gentlemen come to visit us and we received orders to put on our best clothes as those were the gentlemen most concerned in giving them to us. Mr. Macpherson came with them, and I think this was his last visit to us, for the authorities disliked his coming near us and he was obliged to discontinue his visits in consequence.

A day or two afterwards a rumour was afloat that an English Colonel and some other officer had arrived in the town, on their road to a town called Roscen, where all the officers who were prisoners were kept; but those were the only two I ever heard passing through Voronesh. The rumour proved correct, for two officers had arrived and one of them was Colonel Kelly of the 34th Regiment, but who the other was I could not learn. We fully expected a visit and there was much bustle in cleaning the room and ourselves for his coming; but he did not come near us, although he remained in the town three days and must have known we were there. We were all very much disappointed and the men often talked of his unkindness in not seeing us.

Lt. Col. Richard D. Kelly of the 34th (Cumberland and Border) Regiment was 38 years old at the time. He had been commissioned Ensign on the 7th March 1834 and assumed command of the Regiment on the 12th December 1854. On the 22nd March 1855 he was commanding in the trenches when at 11 o'clock an enormous enemy force attacked and Colonel Kelly was shot down and carried off a prisoner.

He survived the war and was promoted full Colonel on on the 30th January 1858.

Our police officer began to be very troublesome, but he suddenly left us, and I don't know the reason. The next we got was a tall, fat officer and, like all Russians in authority, a bit of a bully. He used to make us attend at his quarters for our pay, and would often keep us waiting for hours. On going one day for my pay as usual, I was surprised to see a French Zouave had joined us. I could perceive by the gold lace on his sleeve of his jacket that he was an officer and I soon began to talk with him. He told me that he was a lieutenant and had been taken in one of the sorties. He had been put down as an English dragoon in the Russian account and therefore had been sent to the quarters of the English. In answer to my question why he had not explained to the police master, he said he was tired of marching and was well enough off as he was. He was a tall, powerful-looking man and was a curiosity with the Russians in his Zouave dress.

Zouaves were French colonial light infantry, whose name derives from the Zouaoua tribe from which they were originally recruited. Their uniform was very distinctive, consisting of baggy trousers, short open jacket and small tasselled cap.

One night, as I was returning home, I heard a great noise in the Walki shop close by our dwelling. I went up and found it was this Lieutenant of Zouaves in a row with the Russian police and the keepers of the Walki shop. I looked through the windows and saw the Zouave knocking the police about as he thought proper. He had the appearance of a very strong man and on this night he shewed it. In vain they tried to close with him; he knocked them about like shuttlecocks and soon made his way to the front door. I took the opportunity to walk off to a more respectable distance, for I did not want to be mixed up in any drunken brawl. When he got to the door he tried to make off to our house, but was collared by a lump of a police-man, who had been standing outside; but he picked up the policeman and tried to throw him over the bridge, where he would certainly have broken his bones if he had not killed him, as he would have fallen a good 40 feet into another road that ran under the bridge; but the man struggled so violently that the Zouave lost his hold of him and the policeman, as soon as he found he was at liberty, took to his heels for his life; but the remainder followed the Zouave up close, but was afraid to renew the struggle and the Zouave walked backwards to the house we lived in, facing his pursuers. Two of the guard and the old fellow who sold beer to the prisoners (the same man who used to supply us with an apology for tea in the winter), tried to stop him at the door, but they were soon floored and Mr. Zouave stopped to kick the old man's basket full of beer bottles over and break half of them, and then he bounced into his own room where, I suppose, the Russians thought best to leave him, for they did not attempt to get him out again. After this he turned out to be a regular tartar and the police could do nothing with him. He would go out when he thought proper, and if he met any opposition to his egress at the door he would jump out of the window. He was very fond of drink and when-ever he got the worse for liquor he would be sure to kick the old fellow's basket and bottles about the yard until, at last, when the old man would see him coming he would pick up his ware and run as hard as his legs would carry him.

A short time after this, as I came in one evening, I found all the prisoners standing outside our dwelling and two or three police officers trying to get them into some sort of order. I soon found out that the police master had sent for us and that we were to have our names taken down and sent to England, preparatory to an exchange. This was joyful news and we were all marched off to the police office where, after remaining some time, the Police Master made his appearance and two or three clerks with him. The sailors were sent for in haste and the clerks commenced writing our names in three different books with the date and place of our being taken, the number of our regiment and whether we were wounded. We had to sign our names in each of the books and the clerks were at work all night, but they were very slow coaches. The police master told us he expected we should be off from there in about seven weeks, but both him and us were greatly disappointed in this.

Deserters arrived on almost every Sunday and, the house being full, they were put in a stable where, if possible, the fleas were more numerous than in the house. This stable got the name of 'The rams' nest'—and a nice lot of rams there was in it.

As the summer advanced the weather became tremendous hot and the fleas were swarming everywhere; by night or day there was no rest from them. Many times I have risen off our makeshift bed and took my old coat into the passage hoping to avoid them, but they were as numerous in the passage as in the straw of the beds. Sometimes I have got down into the yard, but go where I would I could not escape them. We used to sit up very late on purpose to keep them waiting for their supper, but I think we got the worse of that movement for they would bite the harder and oftener. I have laid on the old bed for hours in the daytime watching them come through the interstices of the coarse canvas, and would wait patiently until I caught some of them hopping about on my clothing when I would give chase. Unless they were very young and small I generally caught them, for the old, full grown ones could not get through the canvas so easily, and I often used to pull them out when they were half way through; but the young, small ones used to pop through before I was properly aware of it and so escape me.

Through the heat of the summer we generally laid in our shirts and through the night there was the continual slapping noise made by the men bringing their hands down on their bodies or legs with a clap where the fleas were regaling themsleves; and they were pretty sure of catching some of them, for they were too thick to miss them. I have caught scores of a night by this method, but they must be awful things to breed for the more we killed the more numerous they became; but I rather think they were enemies of the lice, for the lice were not so plentiful though we could always find a straggler or two. At last, one morning, we set to work and cleared off all the straw from our old bed and threw it away and laid down on the boards, after which for some time we got on better, but they soon found fresh hiding places and served us out worse than before—I suppose in revenge for their temporary banishment.

One Sunday morning I was surprised at the arrival of Sgt. Noseley of the Rifles (the Sergeant who Mr. Duff and I carried off the field at Inkerman). I was astonished for I never thought to see him alive again being shot through the body . . . He was taken into the 'Staff Room', as we called it where O'Neale and the two cavalry sergeants stopped. In a few days he was well dressed in black undress uniform and a smart, good-looking fellow he was.

In a week after, my old comrade Sgt. Surridge of the 49th came up, and I went to the police master to meet him and we had a spree that day; but Surridge continued sickly and in a few days was obliged to go to hospital again, and he never had his health properly while we remained in the country. He got some cloth and a pair of boots served out to him and he sported silver lace stripes on his trowsers.

The men had of late been getting themselves into scrapes, and at last some fellows chased a lady into her own house. This was the climax, and the police master made his appearance the next morning and had us all assembled in the yard. He talked away at a great rate, with violent gesticulation, and through the interpreter we were given to understand that we were confined to the barracks. Even as he spoke a sergeant's guard marched into the house and sentries were soon placed on the door and front windows. The police master enquired for all the non-commissioned officers, and we were all brought to the front. He told us that we should exercise our authority there the same as in our regiments, that some of us would be placed in each room, and that we should be responsible for the conduct of the men, and that the Sergeant Major (O'Neale) should be in command, and any man that would not obey his and our orders was to be sent to the lock-up, and the guard had orders to take any of the men who O'Neale should point out, and they were all to mess together by rooms and by twos and threes.

In consequence of this arrangement I was sent back to take charge of the same room I had been so glad to leave a short while before. For a day or two we got on very well. I got them agreed to mess together, but here was a difficulty: none of them had any money, and the pay though due a long time, had not come. I had a little and took two of the men to market and laid it out. We were allowed to go to market by tens the first thing in the morning, but many when they got there would not come back till nightfall, when they were pretty sure of being locked up.

I was far from being comfortable in this room for, notwithstanding the orders of the police master, obedience would not be given by the men; and one night O'Neale and one of the cavalry sergeants quarrelled and O'Neale gave the other a black eye, and there was a great shindy of course. When the men saw those who were placed in authority doing such things they soon followed the laudable example, and things went on so bad I determined to go back to my old quarters, which I did after a while.

The men found plenty of means of getting drink in, although they were not allowed out. They would bribe the Russians on guard to get it, and I never saw a Russian who could withstand a bribe, especially soldiers. Besides which, the old serf who had charge of the house would bring it in, for a reward of three copecks and a glass of the spirit, or he would pass one of the sailors out of the door to fetch it for a similar reward, and yet the police officer used to wonder how the men got drunk.

On the first night of the guard being placed over us the sentries began to make that horrible noise that I have described before; a yell that would frighten Old Nick himself, and would not let anyone sleep within a reasonable distance. The sergeant of the guard was requested civilly to put a stop to such music but he would not, and the men took the management of it upon themselves, and, as soon as the sentry began to yell, he would find himself saluted with a jug of water or a dozen potatoes or some other missile from the open window (for all windows were left open through the heat of the weather). The old sergeant bounced first into one room then into another but could not find out who had done the deed and, at last, the sentries found it was best to keep quiet. This game continued for several nights until the Russians all knew how to conduct themselves when they came on guard over English Gentlemen.

As we could not get out of the house we made all kinds of games for amusing ourselves in the evening in the yard. 'Buffet the Bear' was the favourite game, leapfrog and many others that I don't know the name of.

We had a sailor join us of the name of Dove, a little fellow, but continually doing some mischief, in which he was ably assisted by another little fellow by the name of Richardson, also a sailor; and there was a man of the 13th Light Dragoons of the name of Warren, a good tumbler, dancer, tailor or anything else that was required. There was several others whose names I forget, but among them they kept all hands alive and the noise in our yard of an evening resembled the noise in the playground of some large school, and many respectable people would come into the yard to witness our games.

After the games we would have dancing, and we had some very good dancers. I have often seen respectable Russian women beg to join in with the men, but very few of them could dance a polka or waltz or schottisch and generally made a mess of it.

After the dancing there was generally a drinking match in some of the rooms, which would usually last until daybreak, unless it was suddenly brought to a close by a general row, which was often the case. In the sailors' room we used to subscribe 15 copecks each every Saturday evening and send for a large bottle of Walki, which would run to just about two glasses each. We would have songs and recitations until the town clocks struck twelve, when it was always stopped, for the sailors never liked such goings on on Sundays, and should any one of them commence singing or whistling any profane song or tune on that day he was soon given to know what day it was and it would be stopped directly.

There was an old Russian officer lived in a cottage at the bottom of our yard. His daughter, a nice-looking woman, took great delight in viewing our pastimes, and she would stand for hours leaning on her husband's shoulder and watching our proceedings.

One Sunday we had another sergeant major of the light cavalry join us, whose name was Smith. He had been injured in the right wrist by a sabre cut at Balaclava. He went into the staff room but I fancy he was not a great favourite there as he was too plain spoken, but the remainder of us liked him very well.

Sergeant-Major Smith, together with his colleague Sergeant Major Lincoln, both of the 13th Light Dragoons, had actually managed to take possession of two Russian guns at Balaclava. They were, however, soon overpowered and taken prisoner.

Somewhere about this time a sergeant of the 68th regiment joined us, of the name of Cooper. He was a tall man but in delicate health. He and me soon formed a friendship, and a very nice fellow I found him; but O'Neale took some dislike to him, and, although the poor fellow was as ragged as a Pole, he never got any clothing.

Sgt. Cooper of the 68th Regiment (the Durham Light Infantry) was taken prisoner with eight others at Inkerman during the fierce fighting round the Sandbag Battery.

There were two other sergeants came up but I am at default as to the times of their arrivals. One's name was Connolly, of the 57th Regiment, and the other Shaw of the 30th.

Sergeant T. S. Shaw of the 30th (East Lancashire Regiment) was also taken prisoner at Inkerman while defending the Barrier. He was later awarded the Sardinian War medal.

Henry the Hussar, whom I left behind at Karkoff, also came up and he brought a portmanteau of clothes with him and a good watch and plenty of money. He used to make a very respectable turnout, but he soon got rid of most of his good clothes and money; but he bought some fine scarlet cloth and had it made into trowsers and, as his Hussar jacket was good, he cut a great dash in his regimentals. He also brought a good supply of English books and was very liberal in lending them.

There were four of the 11th Hussars among us, and one of them, I believe, had received as many as 27 wounds in the charge at Balaclava, but I forget his name. There was also a young man of the 4th Light Dragoons of the name of Fredericks came up. He was a good speaker of French, in fact he could speak it like a native. He was often our interpreter, for the chief clerk at the police master's could also speak French well. Fredericks could also speak German and was soon a favourite with the police master and several gentlefolk of the town. He had presents coming to him from one or the other daily, but most from a lady, who even sent him a bedstead, bed and bedding and a tea service.

During the whole of this time, we the main body had been confined to the house; there was some who could go out at any time, among whom was O'Neale, the two cavalry sergeants, Sergeant Noseley, Henry the Hussar, Fredericks and one or two others. One man, of the name of Bird, of the 8th Hussars, was taken by a gentleman to his country seat, upwards of 300 versts from Voronesh, where he stopped for a long time, living like a gentleman; but when he came back he had much trouble to get his pay for the time he was away. In fact I rather think that he never got the whole of it.

The young fellow deficient of an arm (Lucas of the 4th Light Dragoons) was also a great favourite with some of the gentlefolks in the town, and I have often known them to send for him to dine or to a ball. Corporal Walsh of the 7th Fusiliers was also a great favourite at one house and was continually invited. Then my little comrade of the 4th Light Dragoons (Farquharson the trumpeter) was an especial favourite of several young ladies, and they would often come and fetch him away.

We lost our officer one day quite suddenly, and I believe because of some trouble which he had had with one of the prisoners and the police master, and was sent in charge of some recruits to the Crimea. His place was supplied by a thin little fellow, who used to bring the pay into our yard by five o'clock in the morning, as much too early for us as it had generally been too late, for this was the time when we could best get a little sleep, as the main body of the fleas would beat a retreat when daylight appeared and only leave a few skirmishers behind to harass the enemy.

One morning he came to our room and hallooed for us to get up and come for our pay. Most of the men went, but I and a few others remained and tried to finish our doze. Presently he came back and took hold of my legs and nearly pulled me off the old bed. I got angry and made a kick at him. He wanted to know if I knew he was an officer, and ordered me to come down for my pay. This I flatly refused to do and he left the room, but soon after returned with some of the guard to march me off to the lock-up, and there I should certainly have gone only for the interference of some of the men, and it would certainly have served me right had I gone; but this officer was instrumental in getting passes issued to us, so that any good-conducted men could get a pass to go out at any time he wished during the day, but must return by 10 o'clock at night, unless on a very particular occasion.

We had fine sport with those passes, for the officer used to attend in the morning between 9 and 10 o'clock to issue them, and used to take the old serf's word for the character of the men: a good source of emolument for the old serf, for he would give anyone a good character who would pay him 10 or 15 copecks for doing so. By such means many good men were often debarred from getting one as the numbers were limited. To remedy this we would write out passes for ourselves, in English, after the officer had departed. We well knew that not one Russian Sergeant in a thousand could tell the difference between a great A and a bull's foot, and so we would present ourselves and passes to him at the door to go out with as much sang froid as though they were genuine. It was laughable to see the sergeant of the guard look over it, trying to make believe that he could read, and how civilly he would return the piece of paper with, "Good, go on." There was no fear of discovery as long as we could preserve our gravity and get in in time.

We had many deserters arrive now and there was one among them of the name of Lithcoe, a regular scamp. He was a great bully and the men did not like to have anything to do with him, for he was a large and powerful man. He was a tremendous thief. Nothing was safe from him. He often stole the poor fellows' bit of clothing and was sure to make off with any sheepskins that were put outside to air unless there was a good watch put on them. He was flogged once or twice, but it did not stop him and, at last, he was given over to the Russian Police for robbing a man of my regiment of a pair of wellington boots and some sheepskin coats of other people's. I think he was the most foul-mouthed man I ever heard, and I was glad when a resolution was passed in our room not to allow him in, and we never left the room without two or three to watch it and the contents.

There was also a man of the 68th Regiment whom we had christened the Irish Arab. This man was a great drunkard and disgraceful character. He was well known to be a deserter for, when he and his comrade got drunk, they would be sure to quarrel, each blaming the other as being the cause of their deserting, so that they had deserted together. The Arab was determined to go back and in spite of his comrade's advice went and had his name put down when the list was made to be exchanged. After the exchange of prisoners I learnt that he had been sentenced to be shot but afterwards was sent to life imprisonment.

There were two more deserters came up at this time one of whom belonged to the 56th Regiment—I forget his name—but he was a fair haired man and had lost a tooth in the front of his mouth. He used to boast that he had been placed on sentry with another man and had tried to persuade him to desert with him, when he knocked his brains out with the butt of his firelock, and then made his way over to the enemy, where he was ready and willing to take up arms against England, and had offered his services to the Russians but they had refused. I should like to see that fellow get his deserts.

The other was a sergeant of the 42nd Highlanders. He deserted in consequence of getting drunk at Balaclava and losing, or making away with, a sum of money entrusted to him. Being a Scotsman, Crawford, the Trumpet Major, used to talk to him. I never saw a man so cast down. He would never look the other prisoners in the face, and would try and slink away when any of us approached him. As the Rams' Nest, where the deserters lived, was a dirty, noisy hole, Crawford invited him to come into our room to sleep, which the other accepted; but he would never go in until the remainder of the men in the room had laid down and the candle was blown out; then he would go in on tip-toe and spread his sheepskin on the floor and lie down, but with the first appearance of daylight he would get up and go out as noiselessly as he had come in, and they would see no more of him during the day. He detested the deserters and would not associate with them and was ashamed to come among us. I pitied him very much. He had a wife and four children in some part of England, who were drawing a weekly allowance from the Patriotic Fund, which of course would cease as soon as his desertion was known, and his wife and children left desolate.

As they were both Scotsmen, young Farquharson the trumpeter also made friends with this sergeant, whose name was Mitchell and relates how:

"Before we left the poor fellow wrote a letter to his wife. He allowed me to see it and it was a most repentant and affectionate letter. It was entrusted to me to post after my release, and deeply did I regret losing it on the journey home."

We had two more soldiers die, one a cavalryman and the other from the infantry, but I forget what regiments. We all followed at their funerals' which was the counterpart of the first, only that the Roman Catholic priest volunteered his services to bury them, which was accepted.

One Sunday myself and my comrade Way went out for a stroll along the banks of the river, where I observed many light skiffs and canoes made fast along the banks with the oars and paddles in them. I pondered it over a long time and at last concluded that it was feasible. I knew from the English papers that we got regularly from MacPherson that the English and French fleets had possession of the Sea of Assoff and, when I had attended the lady in her English classes, I had seen several maps of Russia and the Crimea and therefore knew that the river Voronesh joined the river Don, and that the Don emptied its waters into the Sea of Asoff.

My plan was to steal as much black bread as possible and conceal it in a wood about 4 versts from the town and on the banks of the river. I chose black bread because of its durability and cheapness. I also intended to have bought a small keg, of which there were plenty in the town, to keep water in, should I be fortunate enough to reach the sea. I intended also to have bought some old Russian clothing and to have left the house privately about 1 o'clock and gone to the river and stole one of the skiffs, then row down to the wood and take in my provisions, and then make the best way onwards, travelling at night only and hiding myself and boat during the day in the long rushes in the stream; or if there should be none, I could sink the little boat in the shallow water close to the shore and hide myself and the oars in some place on shore.

I knew I could not take the wrong route as the stream always flows the one way—to the Sea of Asoff, there being no tide. After reaching the sea I intended to trust to providence to fall in with some English or French ship or gunboat. As there was no such thing now as calling the roll of the prisoners in the house, I was sure of having two or three days start before I was missed, and then I thought they would not think of the river. The only difficulties I could see were the chance of discovery when passing those large towns on the banks of the Don, as there would be sure to be plenty of traffic there, by day or by night, and, secondly, the want of a comrade to take a turn in pulling and watching.

I mentioned my plan to my comrade Way, but he would have nothing to do with it, although he owned it was feasible. I next spoke to a man of the 4th Light Dragoons of the name of Thomas King. He had once belonged to my regiment but had bought his discharge, and, some time after had re-enlisted in the 4th Light Dragoons. When I explained my plan he eagerly closed with me as my companion in the endeavour and it was determined that, if the exchange did not take place before the autumn, we would be off, sans liberte. We talked over and matured our arrangements every evening in the yard and saved money in readiness, fully determined to make the trial if the exchange turned out to be a hoax, as we all thought it would.

Eatables had got to be even cheaper than before. We could get half a sheep for 15 copecks (about 6 pence), eggs for 2 copeck and good ham for 6 and 7 copecks per pound. Vegetables, too, were very cheap and we had plenty of new potatoes, carrots and cabbages. Turnips were scarcer and not good, and onions quite the contrary. Fowls, 15 copecks each and turkeys 25 and 30 copecks. Bread continued the same price, but fruit was very plentiful and cheap, but though it was always very good looking the taste did not come up to the appearance, for it had always a peculiar, sharp tang whether apples, pears, plums, cherries, as though it was not properly cultivated. Water melons and sugar melons were piled high about the market in piles like cannon shot. They were very plentiful and cheap, for I could buy a water melon as large as a good sized bucket for 3 copecks. They were very nice and I ate a great many of them. We found a good substitute for mustard, which was horse radish, ground fine like flour and when mixed with vinegar was very good. I lived like a fighting cock, as the saying is, and got so dainty at last that I fancied ham and eggs did not agree with my stomach and I must needs have fowls for a change.

In this way twelve long weeks passed since the taking of our names for exchange, and we had all given it up for a bad job, when one day our hopes were revived by the police master sending for us to his own house where, through Fredericks, he informed us that something was wrong with the last list and that he must send a fresh one, and we should be able to leave the town in seven weeks. He also told us that if there was any deserters among us the Emperor Alexander had given them liberty to stop where they were until the war was over, when he would intercede with the British Government to get them a pardon; that they should still have the same house, room and privileges and pay for any man who thought proper to stop in the country. If any man, knowing himself to be a deserter, should not like to own to it before his own countrymen, he could come and privately tell the police master and have his name put down to stop in the country.

We were all in high glee and began to leave off talking about effecting our escape. The papers were sent off at 12 o'clock the next night.

One of the sailors was taken ill and laid about the room for a day or two but, getting worse, went to the hospital and died in about a fortnight after. All the sailors determined to follow him to the grave, and I also, and we did not expect the remainder of the soldiers would come; but when we got down to the hospital we were joined by nearly all the soldiers and the funeral was the same as the others, except that the sailors walked first and the soldiers brought up the rear, and we had, as on former occasions, plenty of spectators.

One day I was standing with some of the sailors at one of the windows of our room and, looking out in the street, we saw two of the sailors coming home from a walk. They were met close by our house by two Russians, one of whom was drunk and the other leading him. The drunken man was tall and powerful looking and nothing would stop him but he must kick up a row with one of the sailors, a little fellow of the name of Richardson. The Russian went to him and called him a dog and then spat on him and then tried to strike him. But, to his great surprise, he found the little sailor jumping round and hitting everywhere but where he expected, until at last Johnny Russian had got enough of it and fairly ran away to the great amusement of us and a young Russian gentleman who lived opposite and had been watching the whole concern from his window.

In another house opposite to ours there lived a young lady, a very pretty one too, and by all accounts she was very good and charitable to the poor. We often saw her as she left her house, and I believe she had married since our arrival. But she died, and on the day of the funeral we were all at the window to see the procession. I was surprised to see the lid off the coffin and the corpse dressed more like a bride than a dead body, with a wreath of flowers round her brow and a bunch of flowers on her bosom, with the hands clasped, or rather crossed, on them, exposed to the gaze of the vulgar crowd. Four men carried the coffin by long white bands that passed underneath it, and one carried the lid. There was several priests chanting the service, and several censers with the incense, and several lighted tapers in a kind of lanthorn fixed by the bottom on a long rod. The people flocked to the corpse and many of them, both men and women, kissed her, and there was plenty of crossing and mumbling: prayer, I suppose. It certainly was a queer way to bury a young and pretty woman.

One evening there was a tremendous shindy among the staff. O'Neale and Troop Sergeant Major Smith were the chiefs but the others aided and abetted; but O'Neale would not turn out and fight for it as he was wanted to do; but this was queer work again for a person who wished to be in authority. This evening was the first time of my hearing O'Neale's account of his being taken prisoner. I got the tale first from Crawford and afterwards from King as the way O'Neale himself had told it to them on the road up country, and others who came up at the same time confirmed it, and what I have since heard from other quarters I do not doubt the truth of it; if it's true I have no doubt but that O'Neale was either a deserter or taken by his own negligence.

He was regimental sergeant major of the 44th Regiment, and by his own account, upon the regiment arriving before Sebastopol, he was sent with a company under the command of a captain and subaltern one day on outlying picket, before the batteries were built or properly commenced. About an hour before daylight he was sent by the officer to call in some of the sentries, but he missed one man and wandered about to find him. At last he saw a man not far off, whom he took to be the missing man, and called to him and told him to come up. The man had answered, "I can't come, I have a wounded officer here," in good English. He went down to tender assistance to the man to get the wounded officer when, all of a sudden, four or five men jumped up off the ground and took him prisoner.

It is my opinion that, either O'Neale deserted or that he went poking around the picket where he had no business to be and wandered off too far from his own lines and was taken; and yet this man, on his return, got a commission, and he told me himself that he was recommended for a medal for distinguished conduct.

While we were discussing this yarn of O'Neale's in the yard a great many of the men assembled round us and took part in the argument, many of them confirming the words that Crawford told me, having heard O'Neale tell the tale themselves. On the next day the house was full of it and each man appeared interested in it. I think that O'Neale must have heard of our discussion and opinion, for I happened to meet him the next morning and he bid me 'Good morning' in a very bland voice. A piece of civility he had never deigned to do before and which only served to confirm my suspicions and make me believe that he was alarmed at the tone of our argument. Cooper also told me that O'Neale had been very civil to him this day, though they took not the slightest notice of him before, and Cooper was of my opinion as to the cause of the remarkable change.

Newman and his colleagues did O'Neale a grave injustice. Farquharson and Parkes of the 4th Dragoons had met the man who had lured O'Neale to his capture. Shortly after their own capture, after the Charge, they had met an Englishman helping the Russians, who, trying to excuse his actions to the two Englishmen, claimed to be an American making his way from Portsmouth to South America when he was taken by the press gang, served on the *Diamond* and then deserted to join the Russians when the Frigate came out to the Black Sea.

"You're a dammed liar," said Parkes, "because there is no such thing as the press gang in England nowadays. You're a spy and a scoundrel."

The regimental records of the East Essex Regiment

merely record that Sergeant Major O'Neale was taken while withdrawing advanced pickets.

Sergeant Major Francis O'Neale was commissioned ensign on the 6th November 1855, adjutant on the 1st February 1856 and Lieutenant on the 30th November 1860.

One day we had the Adjutant General of the Russian forces come to inspect us by the order of the Emperor preparatory to our departure. We (the proper prisoners) were fell in in one part of the yard, and the deserters in another. He only looked at the prisoners and did not go near the deserters. He again offered the same conditions to those who liked to stop and gave orders for us to be clothed before starting.

In a few days after we were all marched to a place where a great many tailors were at work, making clothing such as we had often seen the Russian recruits wear. We were all clad in long grey overcoats, and a pair of rough black trowsers. They also gave us caps and stocks but we soon threw them away. The next day we each had a pair of boots, and a rough Russian shirt.

These grey coats had a yellow diamond on the back to distinguish the prisoners, but in other respects they were the standard Russian issue.

We were all ready to be off, and at last the happy day came, but previous to our departure we were all marnched down to the police master's in our new outfit for his inspection. Before leaving he bid us adieu and pointed out some of his favourites to the officer who was to have charge of us on the road, especially recommended them to his notice as well-conducted men. He then said he hoped, when we reached England, we would give him a good name, and being assured that we would he appeared much pleased. He came to our house the next morning to see us start and we were fell in in the yard with our bags and bundles. He told us, through Thompson, that the officer had orders not to wait on the road and, if any man got drunk and missed his passage, he would be marched back again to wait for the next exchange, and any man riotous or disturbing the peace was also to be marched back for a like purpose.

There was a tremendous string of waggons waiting for us, each with two horses. They were brought to the gate one at a time and two men mounted each.

Despite the encouraging promises of the Police Master, deserters were now and had been treated with the greatest contempt by both sides. Whilst in captivity some of them had been chained together in gangs and compelled to sweep the street. Now, with their companions leaving for England, their future was bleak.

CHAPTER NINE

Return
August–October, 1855

THE CAMPS OF THE LIGHT, 2ND AND 4TH DIVISIONS

The place was much altered since I left and had I been left to myself I should never have found my way to the Light Division....

We soon left the town behind us. We found the roads very dusty and the wind was high and blew it in our faces, and we were like so many chimney sweeps at the end of the day's journey, through the black dust settling on us, and at night I was glad of the chance of getting into a large tub of water.

On the second day we reached Stariosko, where I left my little comrade ill when coming up. The rain came down in torrents all this day and we were wet through before we had been two hours on the road, and we had several miles to climb as the roads were so heavy through the rain that our cattle could not draw us up. I lost the sole from one of my newly issued boots and the other was fast giving way before we got up the first of the hills and, by the time we got in at night, I was quite barefooted, although I stole some of the old peasant's cordage to tie the soles of my boots to the uppers.

We travelled at a good speed, having fresh horses and waggons waiting for us in different villages. Nothing particular occurred during our journey to Karkoff, which we reached in seven days from the time of our departure. Our officer was a tall, good-looking fellow and thought a great deal of his personal appearance and, just before we entered the town, he got out of his waggon and one of the soldiers held up a large looking-glass for him while he made his toilet in the road before he made his appearance before the belles of Karkoff.

As we entered we had to pass a kind of square or promenade, on which there was a regiment of infantry drawn up in line and a procession of priests in full dress blessing their colours previous to their starting to join the army in the Crimea. We were drove through the town to a prison on the far side, where we were put in a large room and were told to remain two or three days. We all wanted provisions and I wanted to get change for some notes, for I had 14 men's money and could not get change before. Small change is very difficult to get in Russia, and there is regular money changers in the market places, who sell their small change at different rates according to the money market. I have paid as much as four copecks for change of a rouble note and sometimes shopkeepers off whom I have been purchasing would charge for changing a note.

The keepers and the guard at the prison would not let us out and we assembled round the door in a crowd. Somebody gave the word to charge and out we went in spite of their exertions. During our stay there was no more opposition to our going out.

I went and purchased what provisions I wanted, but could not get any change as the hour was late and the market mostly closed. I had to go again the next morning for the same purpose, and then return and serve it out to the men. After which me and Surridge cleaned ourselves and went for a stroll in the town. It was Sunday and the shops were closed, and we were objects of curiosity to the different congregations coming out of church.

We met Nettleton in one of the streets, who told us that he had met an English lady, who had invited him to come to her house and bring some of his comrades with him, and he shewed us the lady's address and asked us to go with him. I did not half like Nettleton after his behaviour to me and the others in this town on our road up country, when he and his comrades refused to share their victuals with us, and I would not go, but Surridge consented and tried to persuade me to go with them. While we were arguing the point in the street, two young gentlemen came up to us and asked us, in French, to go to dinner with them. We had another argument about the propriety of going with them and at last consented to go. They seemed pleased to get us, and we were soon ushered into a good suite of rooms.

Neither of the gents could speak much French and I was about level with them, but we managed to make each other understood pretty well. While the dinner was getting ready we were regaled with paper cigarettes and Walki, but the Walki almost burnt my tongue out, so hot had it been made with capsicombs. The dinner was cold but good, and a dessert of melon and apples and hot Walki. We all stopped about an hour after dinner and, as I wanted to get away from their scorching liquid, I got an address from Nettleton and, shewing it, told them we had to meet a lady in Moscow Street and asked them to direct us to it. They enquired the name of the lady and, when I told them, they all declared they knew her (I believe her name was Mercroft, but I really forget, although I had her name and address for a long time). Our hosts volunteered to show us the street, which they did and, pointing to the house we wanted, they shook hands with us and took much trouble to impress their names on our memories and then they left us, and their names I have quite forgotten.

We found the lady for whom we were in search and were all warmly welcomed. She was a widow and had been the wife of some Russian gentleman. There was a young woman in the room, whom she introduced to us as her only child. She was a fine looking and pretty girl and received us very kindly. They wanted us to have tea and, on our declining, the elder lady produced a decanter and glasses and a beautiful melon and a box of cigarettes. We sat and chatted for some time, we making ourselves quite at home. I observed the young lady looking from the window several times, and the old lady gave us to understand that she was looking for her sweetheart, which piece of intelligence caused a little blushing.

Presently a knock came at the door and the young lady hastened to open it, but it was not the sweetheart that knocked but a great fat priest, who said he had heard that there was some English soldiers in the house and should very much like to see them. He was allowed in and soon made himself quite at home and I saw that he liked both eating and drinking and smoking. He asked us many curious questions through the interpretations of both ladies, and we humbugged the old gentleman finely, but he appeared much pleased with his visit.

At length the expected sweetheart appeared, and I found him to be a little, insignificant, long-nosed, ugly fellow. He was much surprised at the addition to the company, but soon got alongside of his lady love and appeared to be tolerably happy; but I took it into my wise head that he had a hard cheek to come courting such a pretty countrywoman of mine and he so ugly, and I wished him everywhere but where he was.

In the course of the conversation the elder lady told us that she had not seen an English newspaper for some years and that it would be a great treat to get one. I promised to send her some when I got to England. The ladies were very thankful and the younger one proceeded to write down their address, but somehow made a fine mess of it. Ugly then tried, but likewise failed. I then offered my services, which were accepted, and I crossed over to the young lady who had the writing materials. Ugly occupied the next chair to her at the table, and I could not get to write as he stopped the way to the table. I civilly requested him in French, which he understood, to let me have his seat. He left it very slowly, as though he didn't like it, and I popped into his place by the side of the young lady, who could not get out without my moving, as she was in a corner and I in the road. After I had wrote the address I kept the seat and soon got into an animated conversation with my pretty prisoner, while Mr. Ugly sat on the other side of the room and looked as discontented as possible. He was much put out and gnawed his fingernails with vexation and, to make him more comfortable, the old lady laughed at him. He couldn't stand this and got up and left the house, and my pretty countrywoman clapped her little hands in high glee at his mortification. The old priest also enjoyed it and laughed heartily.

We stopped there some hours and I found myself rather unwilling to leave; but the young lady was obliged to be off too, as she had a situation as lady's companion in some high nobleman's family. When we were about to depart the elder lady made us a present of two roubles, saying she was sorry she could not afford more as she was nearly dependent upon her daughter's exertions. In vain I assured her we were not in want; nothing would suit but that we should take the money. I felt that I could not take the money myself so left the room and was soon followed by my companions; but we had not descended one flight of stairs when we were called back and made to promise to call back tomorrow if we did not march. We promised to do so and took our departure.

We rambled about the town for some time and, seeing a kind of show in the market place, we determined to see what was to be seen inside, and we crossed the long wooden bridge to go into the show. As we were crossing the bridge some officers stopped us and one of them, who spoke French, commenced questioning us about our treatment while in their country. We soon were the centre of a mob of people who listened with greedy ears to the officer's explanation to his companions. They all appeared to be much pleased at the good account we gave, and the officer assured the bystanders that he had heard from undoubted authority that their prisoners in England had been treated with great kindness and, on going away, he asked us, if we went to the Crimea again, would we use the bayonet, the poinnard or the knife upon the wounded any more. I replied that the English and French never sought to destroy the wounded until they themselves commenced it at the battle of Inkerman. He replied that their papers, which were always true, said that the English commenced it and that it was the work of barbarians and not Christians.

I began to get vexed, especially as he translated our conversation for the edification of the numerous spectators, and I told him that his journals were liars, that I had been at the fight at Inkerman and saw a little of it and would believe my own sight. We should, I believe, have come to a squabble only at that moment a fine open carriage with two outriders and two postillions came dashing through the assembly, and, seated beside two other ladies, we beheld our young hostess, my pretty countrywoman. She pointed us out to her companions and the whole of them bowed to us as they passed, a bit of civility that I think gave us a rise in the opinion of the officers, for they bid us 'good day' in French and Russian more civilly than I expected and moved off.

A good many of the mob followed us to the show and some of them, I suppose more curious than the rest, followed us inside, where they bothered us with questions that we could not understand. We were entertained with tumbling and sleight of hand tricks, but they were all old to us, and a kind of Punch and Judy pantomime. It was late and dark when we came out and made our way to the prison where, on our arrival, we heard that Madame Tomasin and Mrs Harvey and Miss Hardcastle had been and gone again. They had behaved with their usual kindness and Madame Tomasin had been busy doctoring and binding some of the men's arms and legs; for some of them, before we left Voronesh, had taken a fancy to have their limbs marked by a sailor deserter from a man-of-war, and the ink must have been very bad for the places marked gathered, festered, and some of the men were cripples for weeks in consequence. Madame Tomasin had sent for ointment and bandages and turned up the sleeves of her dress and turned to doctoring properly. Between them the ladies had brought some tea, sugar, shirts, stockings and books, but, before they went away, they were greatly insulted by the Irish Arab, for which he got a tremendous trouncing as soon as the ladies departed.

On the next morning the things they had brought were distributed by lot, as there was sufficient quantity to give each some. My lot was some tea and sugar, which I gave to one of the sailors who was sick and, as we were not to march on this day, myself and Surridge, Nettleton and my little comrade Farquharson, the trumpeter, went out. As this was Monday there was much bustle in the town. We had a good look about the place, and I was much pleased with some of the pictures we saw of the war. One especially, shewing the attack of the combined fleets upon the batteries of Sebastopol. There were either five or six of the largest ships blown up, and the water completely covered with pieces of wreck and men clinging to the pieces.

This was the great bombardment of the 16th October 1854, when the combined British and French fleets had bombarded Sebastopol in support of a land attack. It was signally unsuccessful.

I also saw several caricatures. One shewed our own little Queen and the Emperor of the French leading a charge of cavalry. Our Queen dressed in Hussar jacket and a helmet with a long drawn sword and sitting astraddle on the horse, which so disarranged her petticoats as to show that she wore long black boots up to her knees with tremendous spurs in the heels. I could not understand the reading at the bottom, though I have no doubt it was far from complimentary by the pleasure it afforded the Russians, who were very eager to show it to us and make us understand it.

We went to an eating house to dine and in the afternoon we went to visit our kind hostess of the day previous. She received us very kindly and we stayed with her for some time, but the younger lady was not present and we did not find the place quite so attractive as on our first visit.

When we left we went sauntering down the streets and met one of the sailors, a little man called Ned, who joined the company with us in our stroll. We went down the main street and had just passed a very large building, conspicuously marked as the Hotel de Sinope, when several people in the street called us to stop and mentioned the word 'Officer' repeatedly, and pointed to the hotel. We looked but could see nobody and turned to resume our walk when we were again called and, looking round, saw the officer of our escort in full dress. He called us back and asked where we were going. Of course we told him we were going home, viz, the prison. He asked us to come in and in we went. We went up two or three flights of stairs and were shown into a large, handsomely furnished room, where we saw eight or ten great strapping officers of the Russian Militia and several well-dressed and tolerable-looking young ladies. There was a harp, two clarinets and a violin at the far end of the room and the whole party looked very much as though they were enjoying themselves. We were introduced by our officer to the others, one of whom asked our officer if we understood French. The officer replied that we could not, but I interrupted to say that I could, a little. I was great friends with this six foot officer of the militia directly, and his first questions were whether I could dance, and, without waiting for a reply, he pulled me along to where the ladies were assembled around the musicians. On pulling one of the fair damsels out of the ring he said something to her in Russian and told me in French that she was a good sweetheart. He then took another of the young ladies himself and clapped his hands together for the music. The musicians struck a good polka and, before I could prevent it, I found myself and partner whirling about among the tables and chairs.

It had all been done so suddenly that I had no chance of explaining that I could not dance, and I felt the blood run to my face at the thought of the ridiculous figure I was cutting, and I was half inclined to be vexed, but as we went farther down the room I caught hold of my little comrade Farquharson and shoved him into my place, for I knew he was a good dancer.

My Long Acquaintance, the officer, whirled his partner about in high glee, upsetting the chairs and stools at a fine rate, which appeared to give him great pleasure; but at last he got tired and led his lady back to where he found her and then came to us. Our officer asked us what we would have to drink and told us at the same time to have tea.

"Yes," says my new Long Friend, "have some tea, and a bottle of rum in it."

"No, no," says our officer, "you'll get drunk", and then added in Russian that even I could understand. "Those English are devils when drunk".

The tea was brought and poured out and we seated ourselves to partake of it, when my Long Acquaintance gave us a sign not to drink it, and he went away to the ladies, one of whom soon came up and began flirting with our officer, who was sitting down with us. She enticed him away to one of the windows at the end of the room and then my Long Friend came up again and pulled a bottle out of his pocket, which he soon emptied into our tea and told us to drink it up quickly, and we soon obeyed orders and found the rum very good. As soon as we finished we were regaled with cigarettes and some more dancing, and one young lady with a good voice favoured us with a song, accompanying herself on the harp.

Then there was a general dance, all the officers and ladies and my little comrade, who stuck to his partner through all the dancing. After this some more tea was called for, and the same trick again got our officer out of the way while another bottle of rum was distributed in the different tumblers. The

Russians always drink their tea out of tumblers. We did not swallow this as we did the first, but were going to have a smoke and enjoy it. One of our men got up from his seat to light his cigarette when our officer popped into the seat and took hold of the glass of tea and was doubtless going to swallow the whole of it at one draught when he found himself nearly choked by the strength of it. He got into a great rage and wanted to have the contents of the other glasses thrown away, but we saved him the trouble by drinking it, to the great amusement of the long fellow.

The Long Officer then told me he was on his way to the Crimea and said perhaps we should meet one another again, and asked if I should kill him if we met in battle. I answered that I would if I could, an answer that appeared to please him very much and he translated it to the others and told me he would do the same by me if he could, and we shook hands upon it, he telling his companions that I was a good soldier, could drink and dance today and fight and die tomorrow.

He wanted us to have some more rum, but our officer interfered this time and could not be trapped away again, and at length gave us to understand that we were to march on the morrow and had better be off. He called for the reckoning and found that the tea alone was one and three quarters of a rouble, a sum he liked not to pay, and he civilly asked us to pay the bill between us; but our long friend took the matter up and was not sparing in his abuse for calling five men to treat them and then wanting them to pay, and at last he paid the whole of it. I don't know how we should have got on if he had not, for I do not believe we had so much money among us. Our officer himself conducted us to the door, fearful, I suppose, we should get any more rum and then gave us much admonition not to get any more drunk as we went home, bade us good night and we left him.

About ten o'clock the next morning we resumed our march,

but could not get on as fast as previously owing to the authorities being unable to procure horses, and we had to continue our journey on bullock waggons. About three o'clock in the afternoon we reached the village where I had passed such an uncomfortable night on the way up the country. We halted in front of the old miserable roadside prison and had to wait some time for a relief of waggons. There was a burly-looking man, a kind of chief of police in the village, wearing a piece of narrow gold lace around the collar of his uniform coat, who made himself very busy among our party; and one of the 4th Light Dragoons by the name of King, who had consented to try my plan of escape, was standing in the road and in the way of this would-be-somebody, who, instead of asking King to move, struck him on the side of the head to move him out of the way, a compliment that, to his great surprise, was quickly returned and he found himself lying in the road and his nose bleeding profusely. He jumps up and runs off with his nose in his hands, and our officer coming up shortly after, made a complaint of being ill-used. Our officer heard both sides of the story and then got out of his waggon and took the driver's whip and gave Mr. Policeman a sound thrashing as a compensation.

We reached Walka, the town where I was in hospital, that evening and were billeted on the outskirts. Early the next morning we resumed our march and passed through the town and close to the hospital, and struck off to another part of the country, where we had not been, and did not pursue the same road as we came up any further.

We had beautiful weather during the remainder of the journey, but were generally much troubled to get our victuals cooked, as we were always late getting into our billets and early in starting from them. I cannot recollect the names of all the towns we passed through on this road, but I will tell you the principal ones.

After four or five days' march and passing through several large villages and small towns we arrived at Poltavia, a town famous for a great battle fought in its vicinity by the Swedes and Russians. It was dark when we entered and we could not see much of the town by the light of the few miserable oil lamps. We drove through the dark silent streets, scarcely seeing a living soul besides ourselves until we reached a large house at the corner of two large streets. It was empty and we were put into it. On the next day we were told that we would not march until the following day and that the officer was to be replaced by another. He came to bid us good-bye before starting, and asked if every man was satisfied with him while he was in command of us; and on being assured we were very sorry he could not go the whole distance with us, he was pleased and wished us a quick passage to England.

Peter the Great of Russia (1689–1725), to gain access to the Baltic, defeated Charles XII of Sweden in 1700 and formed an alliance with Augustus of Poland–Saxony, who was in turn defeated by Charles XII.

This laid open the way to central Russia and, sweeping down as far south as Poltavia, Charles was finally defeated at the battle there on 27th June 1709, thus destroying forever Sweden's power over Russia in the Baltic.

I went into the town to buy provisions and was struck by the great number of Jews I met. The town was clean, a remarkable thing in Russia, and there was long rows of glass colonnades in front of the principal shops, looking very much like tremendous conservatories. About every 30 yards there was a pair of folding doors, and by the side of each door there was a large tub painted green and a monster mop. I learnt that these things were in readiness in case of fire. There was a tolerable market and many of us bought meat but had a job to cook it; though there was two coppers and a oven, there was no firewood but, at last, we broke up the flooring in one of the lower rooms and thus provided ourselves with firing.

I had a great job of shirt washing here, for I had now as many as four shirts and they were all dirty. We had been told before reaching the town that Poltavia was a fortified town but could not find any fortification. We could see none the night we entered but perhaps the darkness hid them; but when we left the town we were on the lookout for them, but there was nothing like a fortification on this side of the town. I remember seeing a long bank of earth, some miles in length and quite straight like a railway bank in England, on the plains we crossed over on our road to the town. Our waggons ascended to the top of this bank and continued their journey on it for some miles, but it ended as suddenly as it began, and I cannot imagine the reason for throwing up such a bank in such a place, for it must have been 25 or 30 miles from the town.

We had some fine sport in crossing those large, level plains when we were fortunate enough to get horses instead of bullocks, for we would take the whip and reins from the driver and race each other for miles, very often ending by breaking a wheel or axle and sending the passengers flying out of the vehicles. One day we were at this spot and I was driving, a thing I know almost as much of, as a cow of a firelock. Our driver had dropped his cap and had stopped to go back for it, and I drove as fast as I could make the old horses go, leaving the driver to get on one of the rear waggons. On we went, each striving to get in front, when we came to a valley in the bottom of which was a beautiful, shining river, and a rough wooden bridge over it without a handrail or parapet or a guard against going over the side. The ground sloped sharply down to the river, and down we thundered, each striving to reach the river first. I was a bad driver on the plain, but now we went so fast down the hill that I lost all management of the cattle and they rattled on at a tremendous pace. I could see that they would not take the bridge in the centre, and that there would be an upset, and for the life of me I could not help laughing, especially as the sailors at the rear kept roaring out, "Starboard your helm". I jumped off and left my old comrade Way to his fate, who pulled at the reins like a Turk, but all in vain, and in he went; but we saved the horses and waggon from following him by one of the men turning them across the bridge just in time to save their bacon; but I shall never forget how old Way pulled and shouted "Woo, Woo" in English, which of course a Russian horse did not understand, unless he had had a very superior education.

We often came across large fields of melons and pumpkins. Pumpkins were not of much use to us, but we used to pay our respects to the melons. We also passed large bodies of troops making their way down to the seat of war. Nearly all of them wore a small brass cross on their caps, which proclaimed them to be militia. The militia were very numerous in consequence of the new regulations that any man who served in the militia 3 years during the war was to have his freedom. All sorts of men flocked into the militia and there was a great scarcity of men in the villages. In some there was none to be seen but old men and women and children.

During this march we first heard of the battle of Chernaya bridge. It was told to Fredericks very cautiously by a German, and we had a flare-up on the strength of it.

On 15th August the Russians made an unsuccessful attack on the French and Sardinian lines, across the river Chernaya. The Russian losses were very heavy—over 6,000, while the French and Sardinians' were only 1,701 combined.

More important than the actual losses, however, was the damage to Russian morale for, on the 24th August, a message was sent to St. Petersburg recommending the evacuation of Sebastopol.

One night I was billeted at a house where the mistress and her daughter, a young woman, bitterly reproached us with being the murderers of a husband and son, who had both been slain in the attack on the Alma. We found their reproaches anything but pleasant, especially the old lady's and we made the sergeant of the escort find us another lodging.

Several of the men lost their clothing in this part of the journey. My little comrade Farquharson the trumpeter was one of them. We blamed the soldiers of the escort as the robbers, and I think we were not far wrong. Many of our men lost their provision bags and provisions, and others when they would go to their bags for victuals would find them empty. The soldiers were blamed for it all and I think rightly, though we could not catch them in the act. Many of our men had nothing left but what they stood up in, and we kept strict watch on the soldiers to find out the thieves.

Private Wightman of the 17th Lancers recalled:
"Bird (8th Hussars), Cooper (13th Light Dragoons) and Chapman (4th Dragoon Guards) were set upon by thieves. Setting to business in the good English style, they severely punished their antagonists, who bolted." Arriving at Odessa the incident was reported and an officer and six men put under arrest.

The next large town we came to was called Crimenchook, and it took us quite a fortnight to reach it from Poltavia. It was a large town on the banks of the river Dneiper, and I verily believe that two thirds of the inhabitants were Jews. I never saw so many of this distinct race of people together before. Many of our men were billeted among them and could not get them to cook for them or lend them anything to cook with, and our fellows found that their best plan was to take what they wanted and ask permission afterwards. I saw several Jewish religious ceremonies whilst in the town, for it was on the eve of one of their great religious festivals. I also noticed a telegraph wire running into a large house in the town. This telegraph we often met afterwards and found that it ran into Odessa.

Beside the telegraph wire the only thing of note was the bridge over the river Dneiper and the traffic on the river. The bridge was composed of large long baulks of timber, in some cases as many as five deep, floating on the water. The road was made on top of those baulks and the whole was secured by anchors and cables. Some of the pieces of timber must have been 60 feet long, and though the centre part of them would be five or six feet under water yet both ends would be above, so that the pieces of timber must have been bent like a bow with the weight. The river was very wide: I should think much wider than the Thames at London; and the stream was strong, and they must have had good sound tackle, or it would have been carried away by the current. There appeared to be plenty of traffic on the river, for there was plenty of large barges passing up and down and I noticed a great deal of boat and barge building going on on the banks of the river.

Several of our men were taken ill at this place and were received into the hospital, among them was my old friend Surridge, and I was afraid they might miss the exchange in consequence.

Our route from this place was very slow and tedious, for we could get no more horses, except now and then a few who had to keep pace with the bullock. Instead of looking out now for a waggon with a good horse or with two horses when we came to a relieving place, as we used to do, we now looked for a good long waggon with plenty of hay or straw in it, so that we could lie down and sleep if we liked. I generally walked on ahead of the caravan and when I got tired I would sit down and wait until they came up. The Russian sergeants would drive on ahead and when they came to a Walki shop they would enter and order the master of the house not to draw any drink for the English who were coming, and when our men came up they would find the tap stopped and the only way to open it was to treat the sergeants, and many a glorious drink they got by this plan. At length they were not contented with being treated, but tried to make money by their authority, and would order the master of the house to raise the price of the liquor during our short stay and then they would divide the profits between them. This plan was conducted for some time, but became known through the two worthies quarelling when drunk about the division of the spoil. It caused many a row between our men and them and, when our fellows found the tap closed until they chose to pay the price they demanded, they would take forcible possession of the premises and issue the drink at the price they thought it was worth, and the Russians would stare at the quick manner in which the drink would be served and the change given, for the Russians are very slow at such things, and the two sergeants came rather short of their cheap glasses now.

Myself and the old sailor Way now parted comradeship as he was determined to stay on the spree, and I and one of the sailor lads joined as messmates for the rest of the journey. He was a Jew and amused me greatly by his tales of his people and customs.

One day, in the middle of the day, we came to a small town the name of which I forget, but opposite the market place there was a large house that took our attention and, as we were obliged to wait for the relief of waggons, we soon assembled round it and soon after we ventured inside the gates and, no notice being taken, we gradually spread ourselves over the grounds and I enjoyed myself very much. The grounds were well laid out and ornamented with statues, and in the flower beds there was some very good plants. It was a pretty and a beautiful river flowed through it, over which there was a fancy bridge. There was two very big arbours thickly grown with evergreens, and the whole place was the best I have seen in the country.

In the next large town we reached we found it nearly as much populated by Jews as the last one we left. I was billeted at a Jew's house in this town and, because they would not oblige us with utensils and fire for cooking, by the advice of my comrade (the Jew) we rubbed their pots and other utensils with pieces of bacon fat and left pieces of the same in them, and the next morning saw them taken out and broken up as being defiled. While we were in the town an old German Jew told Fredericks, in a whisper and with great caution, that he knew for certain that Sebastopol had been taken, but we did not believe him. An officer of some high rank, for he had an aide-de-camp with him, also told Fredericks that Sebastopol had fallen, but added that it might not be true as there was no official news of it. We were all at great anxiety to get at the truth but could not, for though people in Russia may know a thing well yet they must not speak of it until the account of it has appeared in the gazette.

The next day on leaving the town we got waggons with horses, but only for the first stage. We noticed a very large building as we left the town, surrounded by a garden, which we soon found to be a military college. We travelled very slowly after we lost the horses, and in two or three days' time we reached a small village by the side of the main road. There was a kind of public house at the entrance to the village and before the door stood a large travelling carriage with four horses. Fredericks was soon in conversation with the people who owned it, and found that they were a family who were going to their country residence in the Crimea, but had just heard from the courier, who was in the house, that Sebastopol was taken and the allies expected to advance up the country. They had advanced thus far in their journey, but had now altered their minds and had determined to go back again.

While Fredericks was talking to them in the carriage, I saw a cavalry officer come out of the house and call for a horse in a great hurry and stamp and swear because there was none ready for him. I walked up to him and asked if he could speak French. He replied that he could. I then asked him if it was true that Sebastopol was taken. He looked round very carefully and then said:

"It was taken last Saturday, thank God, and I am the courier with despatches for St. Petersburg."

The horse was brought before he was scarcely done speaking, and he mounted and set off with full speed. I noticed that he wore two brace of pistols in his belt as well as his sword. This piece of news was decisive and, as there was no more waggons to be got that day, we were billeted in the village and all hands went on the spree on the strength of the downfall of Sebastopol. Along the road we joked the soldiers about losing Sebastopol, and made them to understand that the English and French would soon be up where we were then; and after we had got their steam up with this topic we all laughed.

Sebastopol was near to collapse for some weeks before it finally fell. After a most courageous siege lasting nearly a year, it fell on the 8th of September. The French, at noon, attacked the Malakoff Battery, long considered to be the key to the defences and quickly captured it. The British attack on the Redan was less successful, though the Allies won the day.

It was, however, a hollow victory. The gallant defenders

had fled. Before doing so they had fired the place, which raged and burned all night.

The next large town we came to was called Worenscow and as we entered it the peasants, who were driving our waggon, showed us the place where the Russian army was encamped before their departure to attack Silistria. They showed us the places where they cooked and where their artillery laid, and also the place where the Emperor Nicholas stood to review them before they set out on their journey. This was purely a military town. It was well laid out, the streets were long, wide and straight, and chiefly composed of white cottages. Those in the town were chiefly occupied by officers and their families and the long streets leading from the town were occupied by soldiers. There appeared to be at least a dozen in each dwelling.

I was much amused at the method of thrashing adopted here. The corn was spread in a circle and in the middle a strong stake drove into the ground. Two horses were attached to the stake by a long cord, to allow them to reach the outer part of the circle, and a man stood in the centre with a whip and drove the horses round and round. As the horses proceeded round and round the circle the cord wound itself gradually around the stake in the centre and gradually drew them closer and closer to the centre. When the cord was wound up the horses were turned to the 'right about' and made to trot in the contrary way, which gradually unwound the cord again. The mistress of the house was occupied on the outside of the circle throwing the corn into the line of the tread of the horses with a wooden pitch fork.

We resumed our march about twelve o'clock the next day, and I don't remember anything of consequence occurring until we reached a tolerably large village, one day's journey from Odessa. Here we found a great number of troops. Every house was crammed with them and every hay or corn stack was pulled about and formed the sleeping place of scores of them. We were fortunate enough to find a haystack unoccupied and immediately took possession of it. During the night many more troops arrived and at the break of day were all on the move again. We came across several returned prisoners. Those who had been in the hands of the French gave them a bad name, saying that they had to work on the fortifications of Toulon and if they did not complete the task that was given them they got no victuals, but when they did complete the task they were allowed two sous per diem in addition to their rations. They had not their liberty but were confined in a prison when not at work. Those who had been in England gave it a good name, saying they had plenty of victuals and no work and good beds and plenty of money and could get porter and ale.

Some of them told us of their having been taken to some large house in Portsmouth when they landed, and had been treated to plenty of eat and drink. Many of them had learnt a little English and could call for a pot of beer or quarter of gin as well as I could, and appeared much pleased with their visit to England, some of them saying they hoped they might be taken prisoner again.

They had been held at Lewes, Sussex. Private Wightman also recalls this meeting and what the returning prisoners told him:

"Very good stout, very good beer, very good beef. Brighton very good. Russia got no Brighton. Russia no good. Sorry to come back".

Our journey from this place to Odessa was over a large dreary plain with telegraphs by the side of the road. After three or four hours' travelling we caught a view of the Black Sea and the sight was very refreshing to us. We continually met detachments of troops on the road and a quantity of baggage and goods of almost every description. As we came nearer to the town we spied the masts of vessels and shortly after we got on a rising ground where we could plainly see a two-decker lying in the bay of Odessa. The sight was very refreshing, and many were the opinions as to whether it was an English or French vessel.

We passed along a piece of level ground at the bottom of the bay, but between us and the water there was a plantation of young firs and we could not see what batteries and defences the Russians had thrown up along that part of the coast. On our right hand landwards we passed a good park of field artillery and the encampment of two or three regiments of infantry. On entering the outskirts of the town we saw many soldiers throwing up earthworks at the ends and corners of the streets, but made so as to not quite block up the thoroughfare, leaving just enough room for a waggon to pass. Some of our men were of the opinion that they were only temporary and merely made to instruct soldiers in such work.

As we proceeded into the town we saw several large buildings like warehouses filled with troops, and they were all ready for an attack by land. We saw a good many Cossacks galloping about the town and there was no lack of soldiers on the streets, but the place appeared much deserted and the traffic very small for so large a town. We ascended a steep hill and went through a place where there was an immense quantity of hay stacked. The stacks were very large ones; some of them must have been a hundred yards long and broad and high. There was a great many such stacks and I never saw so much hay in one place before or since, and they were building fresh ones in several places and waggon-loads of hay stood ready to be unloaded.

In another place there was a lot of cavalrymen drawing forage for their horses. We heartily wished that our cavalry could pounce upon this vast collection of forage or that the Men-of-War knew of it and knew where it was situated, for a few shells or rockets would have made a fine fire of it.

We were conducted down a fine wide street and stopped in front of a pair of gates opening to the road. Here our journey ended, having taken seven weeks from Voronesh, which when we commenced we trusted to complete in twenty-one days.

> Originally, the Greek 'Odessos', the port of Odessa had been for centuries the Turkish village of Kadzhi-beri. In 1792 Russia annexed the area and rebuilt the little village as the port and naval base of Odessa in 1795.
> The prisoners arrived here about the 26th of September.

We were put in a large house and told that we were not to go out under any pretence, and that our pay would be stopped, and we would be supplied with provisions, and that it should be cooked for us, and if there was any money of our pay not expended it would be given up before we left. We had an interpreter come who damped our spirits with the intelligence that Capt. Duff and many other officers and men had been exchanged the week before and that we should have to wait six or seven weeks. This was a great damper, for we had made sure of being exchanged in a day or two at the farthest.

We found that part of the house was occupied by Turks, chiefly officers, several of whom told us that they had been taken at Silistria and were all more or less wounded; some of them could only get about on crutches. There was an officer among them who was an Irishman and had joined the Turkish army. He still had a great antipathy to all Turks, and several dirty, unmentionable tricks among them soon made us bad friends.

We were here joined by a master's mate and boatswain and Man-of-War's man, all belonging to the navy and had been taken at some place in the Sea of Asoff called Taganroc, where they had been sent on shore to fire some corn and hay ricks. The boatswain and master's mate did not stop with us long for, claiming themselves to be officers, they were sent into another house set apart for English and French officers, but the sailor remained with us.

Following the capture of Kerch in May the allied ships had been harrassing the coastline of the Sea of Azov destroying crops and supplies.

Commander Coker of the Royal Navy built a raft strong enough to carry a 32 pounder gun and named the craft *Lady Nancy*. He put 18 men aboard and towed her to Taganroc on the northern shore of the Sea of Azov.

Taganroc was the town where Alexander I, a legend in his own time, died in November 1825. Taganroc had become a shrine to him and it was even rumoured that he had not died at all but was in hiding.

We were visited soon after our arrival by a little Frenchman who took notes of the wearing apparel required by some of the men who had had their clothing stolen on the road. He also enquired if any of us were sick, and promised to bring a doctor with him in the morning and also to bring tobacco and pipes.

Also we were visited by a good-looking French officer, a prisoner. He was accompanied by some high military officer of the Russians. As they went round the different rooms they came across the Lieutenant of Zouaves. The tall French officer imediately claimed him as a brother officer and Mr. Zouave, having explained the case of his having been sent with the English, was sent from us to quarters set apart for officers. Here a short time after he obtained all his back pay as an officer from the time he was taken, amounting to a good sum; and he gave the Russians plenty of employment to run about and search for him, for he would break out of his quarters and get into the house on the spree. They put a guard over the house, but he bought overclothing and would pass the guards unknown and, when found out at this, he scaled the walls of several gardens until he reached the street. The soldiers and police where continually in search of him and when they caught and brought him to his quarters and thought they had him alright he would be off again before they knew it and they would have a fresh hunt for him.

Our rations consisted of a three pound loaf of good bread daily and a very small quantity of meat and potatoes and onions. The whole of it could not have cost more than five copecks, and we were very indignant at being put on such fare and kicked up a row to know what had become of the remaining fifteen copecks. We could only have one meal per day, and the meal was so small and our Russian cook made a tremendous large copper of soup from it; but it put me very much in mind of the soup we got at Fort Constantine, the first day after Inkerman.

We took notice that the Russian soldiers of our guard were always very busy in our cookhouse peeling the potatoes and onions and assisting the cook, and, when ready, they would be seen, a dozen at a time, with spoon and dish putting our soup out of sight. Of course we kicked up a row and got Mr. Cook turned out and two of our own men put in in his stead, and the soldiers had to keep a respectable distance from our cookhouse in future.

There was a man allowed to keep a kind of stall in one of the cellars of the house to supply us with butter, melons, cheese and garlick'd sausages. He smuggled Walki inside and used to retail it at a price that would soon have made his fortune had he custom enough. He would buy bread from us, for we had more bread than we could eat, and would give us two copecks per loaf for it. He would also buy clothing, and many of the men sold the long grey coats that had been given them, and some sold everything but what they stood up in, and finely did they cheat the old slate keeper. He had no place to put what he bought, only by his side, and when he had bought a coat and laid it down beside him one of the men would steal it and sell it to him again. One day I saw a coat sold six times over to him, and bread was often sold three or four times over, and the game was carried on for a long time before he found out, and when he did he told everyone who came to beware of the English for they were the greatest thieves on the earth.

We generally passed the day playing cards or washing our things and in the evening sang and danced until bed time. We had beds similar to what we get in barracks in England, filled with straw, but they were very lousy, and there were no bed clothes.

We had an officer of the Sappers and Miners join us here, but he merely came to look at us and then was sent to the officers' quarters. The time passed very slowly and miserably and our impatience to be off aggravated our misery. The little French gentleman came as he promised and brought a doctor with him, and he came every morning afterwards during our stay and he used to supply us with tobacco and soap and other things, and when the doctor prescribed for any of the men he would bring the medicine in the afternoon.

One day a whole host of Turks arrived in our yard and all the English got orders to shift their quarters to another house. This we soon did and were glad to get away from our neighbours the Turks. We carried our lousy beds with us and were soon installed in our new quarters, which were much better than the ones we had left, for the house was much larger and we had it all to ourselves. The house faced one of the main streets and we could see a little of what was going on. There was a railing enclosing a piece of ground and we could get a chat through it with the passers-by. We had a fine piece of ground at the back which had once been a garden and served us as a drying ground.

We kicked up another row about the provisions and got it altered so much that we could have two meals per day, our own men cooking.

There was a house in front of ours, on the other side of the road, whose inmates sold some very nice grapes and we used to keep a boy very busy in running to and fro. One day a high officer came to see us and gave orders that we should not be allowed to converse with people in the street, and a sentry was placed outside the railings to keep people from speaking to us. We were very indignant at this for it was our chief amusement. On another day a carriage pulled up in front of our house and a lady and a girl between eight and ten years of age came to talk to the men. The sentry interfered and there was the likelihood of a row in consequence, but the officer of the guard came out and, on the lady speaking to him, he told the sentry to leave her alone. We found the lady to be English and the little girl her daughter and her name was Hunt. She made many enquiries as to how we were treated, and we found it was this lady who sent and paid the doctor for his daily visits and had sent us all the things that had been given us. When told that we had two men very ill in the house she tried to come in to see them, but would not be allowed, but in the evening she sent her servant with boiled chicken soup and other things for the sick.

One morning we were surprised by the unusual bustle in the town. Waggon after waggon passed our house, loaded with furniture and other goods. Carriages heavily loaded and filled with ladies and children galloped past and Cossacks and military officers were riding about in all directions. We wondered what was the matter and when the little Frenchman came he told us that the whole of the allied fleets were in the harbour and they expected the town to be attacked at any minute. We were all very glad to hear it and many climbed the roof of the house to try and see the fun. We waited very impatiently to hear the report of guns, but we waited in vain. Our guard was strengthened and I expect that if the attack had been made we should have been marched into the interior again.

The fleet remained there the whole of the next day and the next, but on the following morning we could hear the sound of a cannonade, but it must have been a long way off. This was the attack on Kimburn, as we afterwards learned.

> The Kimburn Spit is a neck of land jutting out to protect the mouth of the Rivers Dneiper and Bug. It was defended by three forts and seventy guns, under the command of General Kokonovitch.
>
> On the 7th October an allied force of 10,000 men sailed from the Crimea, under the command of the French General Bazaine. They arrived on the 14th and a steam flotilla entered the Dneiper bay. Troops were landed and, on the 17th October, Kimburn fell. The expedition continued up the river Bug and captured Nicolaiv, the Russian naval base 80 miles up the river.

When the fleet departed the inhabitants returned to the town and things appeared to go on as usual. Mrs. Hunt came often to talk with us at the railings and brought shirts and stockings to be distributed to those who wanted them and tea and sugar for the sick. She was a kind-spoken lady and deserved our warmest thanks for her goodness.

One day we were visited by a young man upon crutches. He spoke broken English and gave us to understand that he had been severely wounded and taken prisoner at the Alma, and had been in hospital at Scutari. He had there learnt what English he knew and must have picked up very quickly for he could talk tolerably well. He complained greatly of his treatment during the first part of his captivity. It appeared that he was a military cadet and had not been commissioned as an officer, but, still, in his own country, he was treated as an officer and a gentleman. When taken prisoner he was put down as a soldier in the ranks and our people would not believe him to be anything else. He owned that the surgical assistance he got was good, but complained of being nearly starved, especially when he began to get better of his wounds. He said that he and another man took it in turns to eat the victuals of both, so that one day he had just sufficient and the next none at all. He complained that the tea was made in a greasy copper that the meat had been boiled in and was undrinkable. After some time he had been recognised as an officer by the English, and for the remainder of his stay treated as such, had plenty to eat and was sorry to come away.

In the daytime we amused ourselves by playing cards, walking about the piece of ground in front of the house, cutting pipes out of the soft stone out of which the house and garden walls were built, cutting our names and regiments on the walls of the building, washing and mending our clothes, etc.

In the evening we generally assembled in a large room at the back of the house, where we would sit around the walls on the floor one of our number taking the office of master of ceremonies (generally Warren of the 13th Light Dragoons), who would call upon some one of us present for a song. The individual called upon had to rise and stand facing his audience while he sang, and we would all join in the chorus, making a most tremendous noise. After two or three songs had been sung, the master of ceremonies would generally intimate that the next song would be a dance and invite any gentleman who felt disposed to dance to stand up. He would then pair them off in partners and the trumpet major (Crawford) would strike up a tune on the flute and we would have a polka, sometimes a waltz, a quadrille, schottich or gallop.

After the dance the last person who sang was called upon to amend his call upon another and then, after two or three songs, another dance, sometimes a jig—and thus we would pass the evening until time to retire to rest. The Russian soldiers of the guard would come in and stare at our frolics, and the officer of the guard would bring his chair into the room and sit with us the whole evening, and they always appeared to enjoy the sport and several times told us that the Russian soldiers had no idea of enjoying themselves as we had.

We went on from one thing to another, for a few of us combined together to amuse ourselves and the rest; and Mr. Warren, being a good tumbler, was persuaded to become a pantaloon, and a young fellow of the name of Parker of the 11th Hussars as his comrade Joey. Dresses were made and Warren gave lessons to Parker in tumbling and other tricks, and they would enliven us in the interval between songs and dances. Some of the men set to work one day and made a rough chandelier from some dry reeds, and next day I thought I could make a better one and set to work and soon made a large and tolerably good-looking one from some evergreens out of the garden. It had only eight lights at first, but I improved it daily and soon got one with twenty four and so large as to cover the centre of the room and decorated with small paper flags.

We were not content with singing and dancing but must have a Bal Masqué and enlisted several more into our party to assist us, two of whom were to be transmogrified into women. One was the young man of the 4th Light Dragoons who had lost his arm—Lucas—and the other Corporal Walsh of the 7th Fusiliers, both beardless and able and willing to be turned into ladies, and very good-looking ladies they made, especially Lucas, with a wreath of green leaves round his head. He so much resembled a woman that one of our fellows, who did not know what was going on, enticed him into a corner to kiss him, and what else my modesty forbids me to say; but he got a severe joking about it.

We had a grand masquerade. There were dresses and noses of the queerest pattern as were ever brought to the notice of an admiring audience, and the evening passed over very pleasantly, and the officer of the guard was so pleased this day, especially at a game of cock fighting between dancing, that he gave us a rouble when he left, which was laid out in candles so that we could have plenty of light in the evenings.

This sort of pastime continued a long while. Every morning the programme of the evening's amusement would be written on the walls of the house with a piece of burnt stick and at the bottom were always the words: "Mr. Warren, Manager—Mr. Newman, Architect and Decorator."

It began to get stale at last, although Mrs. Lucas and Mrs. Walsh put on their best smiles to keep the game up, and we could see that we must try something else; and we determined to have a play, but there was a difficulty: none of us knew any plays and we had no books nor could we get any, but Henry of the 11th Hussars remembered a good bit of the farce 'The fish out of water', and what he could not recollect we made up ourselves. He knew the plot of the piece and that was sufficient for us.

'The Fish out of Water', a farce by Joseph Lunn, was first performed on the 26th August 1823 at the Theatre Royal, Haymarket.

Henry was chief manager and director and in two days we had all got our parts off thoroughly. The next day we set to work to knock up a stage and a great job we made of it. We had nothing we could form into scenery but we parted one part of the room off for the stage and formed the side fronts by hanging up some of the grey coats. We got two blankets from the Maltese and made a curtain with then, but with all our ingenuity we could not get the curtain to roll up and were obliged to be content to draw the curtains to the side. We stole the iron gutters from the roof of the house and made shades for our footlights with the pieces, and cut candlesticks out of the soft stone. Our back scene was an old blanket stretched upon a line, and, when this was removed, it showed the double glass doors that opened to the garden, which in itself made one scene. We borrowed a table and two chairs from the officer of the guard and as for dresses we had plenty, apart from women's attire in which we were rather deficient. We could not form an orchestra and therefore Crawford was behind the scenes with his flute.

The thing went off capitally. All the officers came to see us perform and declared themselves much amused. I was a foot-man and in love with the housemaid, Betty (Mrs. Walsh). I forget the names of the other characters as they were ficticious. After our performance Sergeant Connolly and Fredericks came out in 'The Quarrels of Brutus and Cassius', and between acts Mr. Warren and a cavalry man of the 18th or 17th of the name of Cooper came out in a comic song 'Going A-shooting'. Mr. Warren had made a wooden gun and Cooper had enticed a curr of a dog into the place during the day and kept him for the performance. Each of them had a haversack hung over their shoulder for a shooting bag, and Mr. Warren had managed to get a cat somehow, which he buttoned into the haversack with its head out of the top. Mr. Warren made his appearance on the stage first, followed by Cooper with the dog. The dog was obstinate and had to be pulled on with a string round his neck and so round and round the stage in the course of the song, the dog hanging back the whole time as though his life depended on it, and every now and then giving a yell that excited roars of laughter and clapping of hands. The clapping of hands frightened the cat and she got out of the box and ran up Mr. Warren's back at a great rate, and caused more sport and laughter than the dog.

After 'Brutus and Cassius' we had songs and nigger melodies, varied with a hornpipe and other dances and ended up with the National Anthem. The officers made us a present of three roubles and the interpreter, who was present, professed himself highly delighted and promised to bring some of his friends the next time we performed.

Having succeeded in satisfying our audience so well the first night we determined to try again and, as none of us knew not even the plot of any play, we were obliged to turn authors as well as actors, and Henry and I concocted a piece between us which he styled 'The Wicked Country Squire'. We were two or three days getting our parts off and had more characters and therefore strengthened our company with two or three other amateurs, among whom was my little comrade Farquharson. During the day and between rehearsals, we employed ourselves in making a better stage. There was plenty of long reeds to be got, for they used them for the cookhouse fires, and with these we made frames by tying them together, the frames being about eight inches high. These we interlaced with green leaves and boughs so thick that they could not be seen through, and then placed them up for side slips. The front sides were made in a similar manner but much higher, and the back was formed in the same manner, only it reached the whole width of the stage and had a pair of folding doors in the centre. There was a large hook in the centre of the ceiling and to this we tied pieces of string from our stage front and covered them with evergreens, and the chandelier, hanging from the same hook under our many wreaths of evergreen, made the whole look very well indeed. In addition to this we had the Royal Coat of Arms drawn on a large sheet of paper and fixed over the front of the stage, and when everything was complete and the candles lighted it really looked remarkably well.

The large room was completely filled between our own party and officers and the Russian Guard and several visitors. We took care to keep them waiting long enough, and then Crawford tried to make the time as pleasant as possible by giving them several tunes on the flute. Our performance consisted of 'The Wicked Country Squire' in two acts followed by 'The Fish out of Water' in two acts, and between acts and pieces we had nigger melodies, sentimental and comic songs and dances, and concluded with the National Anthem by the whole strength of the company; but I must tell you my part in 'The Wicked Country Squire'. The characters were: The Squire (Henry); Roger, a peasant in love with Violet (Mr. Newman); Philip, a peasant and in love with Emma (Mr. Parker); Old Jacob, a peasant and father of Violet (Mr. Cooper); recruiting sergeant (Mr. Edwards, the corporal who was taken at Inkerman when firing with me); Violet (Mr. Lucas); Emma (Mr. Walsh); Dame Margaret (Mr. Farquhason); recruits, peasants and supernumeraries of the company. The piece opened with a country dance on a village green. Oh, that dance, what trouble and drilling. Old Warren had come to take a few steps in that country dance. During the dance the squire comes upon the green and the peasants cease dancing, but he persuades them to keep on and declares he is happy to see them so happy. He falls desperately in love with my Violet and makes up his mind to get her from me. When the dance is over, the peasants separate and exit. The squire calls old Jack and Jacob and Margaret and enquires very kindly of their worldly comforts. Old Margaret makes a great many complaints, just what the squire wanted, and he promises to call at their cottage the next day to see what could be done for their comfort, but in fact to see Violet. He determined to get rid of me and orders his steward to discharge me and give me a bad character, should anyone else wish to employ me, and sends for the recruiting sergeant. End of Scene 1.

The squire bribes the sergeant to enlist me by fair means or foul, and then goes to visit old Jacob and Margaret, and orders a great many things for their comfort, and proposes that Violet should go to the Hall as servant, which is gladly acceded to by old Jacob and Margaret, but very reluctantly by Violet.

Squire departs and sorrowful interview between Roger (the discharged) and Violet and parents. End of Scene 2.

Interview between Roger and squire ends in reproaches and threats. Village Inn: recruits drinking and playing cards; Roger gets drunk and forgets his sorrow, falls out with sergeant and wants to fight him. Makes friends again and tries to sing, plenty of drink comes in and Roger is led off (but enlisted first) by two recruits and the sergeant, glorious drunk and hiccuping 'I won't go home till morning'. Village green the following morning: Sergeant greatly puzzled to get the recruits into military order before marching off; tender adieu between recruits and sweethearts; heartrending parting of Roger and Violet; end of Act the first.

A period of three years supposed to elapse between Acts. Act 2, scene the first. Village green, evening: enter Roger returned from the wars with crutch and his left arm in a sling and a black patch over his eye, a knapsack on his back and dressed in a ragged suit of soldier's clothes; meets Philip, who does not know him; gets Philip into conversation and finds that the squire has been trying to do wicked things with Violet soon after his departure; the squire had been taken ill and sent off to Italy for the benefit of his health and could not proceed with his designs against Violet during his absence, but had returned this very evening and persuaded Jacob and Margaret to send Violet to the Hall once more. Exit Philip.

Roger determines to go, as he is, to the squire's and beg a night's lodging. He is received by Emma, who does not know him; supper scene between Roger and servants; all retire to rest. Roger lies down in his coat with the crutch by his side. At midnight the squire enters with a lighted candle and in his dressing gown, and vows he will do . . . what you may imagine to my Violet. He passes through the folding door in the back; shrieks and cries for assistance. Roger rises and collars Mr. Squire and drags him out of the bed chamber. A desperate struggle between Roger and the squire, and ends in Roger giving Mr. Squire a topper with the crutch and lays Mr. Squire on the broad of the back. Roger discovered by Violet; tender meeting; Squire believes he is done and sends for Jacob and Margaret and a lawyer and settles a good round sum upon Roger and Violet and then, to his great surprise, finds that his time was not yet done, but will not alter the settlement and determines to go away to another place and turn a good man and be no more a Wicked Country Squire.

The whole of the performance passed over with great success, and we were not a little proud of our turnout; but the interpreter did not like us to sing 'God Save The Queen' and rose and left the room, but declared himself highly satisfied in other respects with the performance.

The next morning, the 21st October 1855 we received intelligence that the Governor of the town and his family and several ladies would honour us with their presence at our next performance; and Farquharson knowing the plot of the play called 'Jonathan Cradford' we determined to perform it, and I and Farquharson was very busy casting the characters and preparing the different parts when, about 10 o'clock, the order came to pack and be off.

'Jonathan Cradford, or The Murder at the Roadside Inn', a melodrama by Edward Fitzball, was first performed on the 12th June 1833.

Farquharson in his account confirms most of the information about the performances, which Newman relates. It seems strange that all this talent should only have flowered in the four weeks of their captivity in Odessa.

We were soon ready and some waggons arrived, loaded with packing cases and, on being opened, was found to contain shirts and boots; one pair of boots and one shirt were given to each of us. The boots were wellingtons and pretty good ones, but the shirts were small. They distributed some money among some of the men as being the balance of their pay after paying for rations, but many of us would not trouble ourselves to take it, thinking we would not have any opportunity of spending it.

Sergeant Surridge and the other men whom we had left behind sick at Crimenchook had rejoined us about a fortnight previously, but Surridge continued very sickly. An Engineer officer took command of us and we were marched through the town to a dockyard on the shores of the bay. Here we were joined by the Turks, but they had to wait until we had embarked. We were put in a large boat and pulled off to a small steamer that lay off the shore, and the English prisoners alone filled it. There was a white flag of truce flying on the flagstaff in the dockyard, another on the small steamer and one in the bows of each of the boats employed in embarking us. The two-decker blockading ship had a large white flag in her fore top mast and the French colours at the mizen peak, while a large merchant steamer kept standing in and out of the bay with a large white flag at the main and the old Union Jack at the mizen.

There was no time lost, but as soon as we were all on board the steamer started, and the English steamer came slowly nearer in. When we got pretty close the boats of the English steamer put off and two or three from the liner. We were soon changed from the little steamer to the English boats and thence to the English steamer. We stood out of the bay, but soon returned and took the Turks on board. We gave the Russians three cheers; and as soon as the little steamer returned to the shore all the white flags were lowered and the truce was ended.

I noticed when we were in the dockyard that a great many vessels of different sizes were sank along the wharf, and I believe it had been done purposely to prevent them being captured. The English steamer was called the Colombo; and we stood out to sea some distance and then anchored for the night. The Turks were not allowed to go below but were obliged to keep on deck, and they revenged themselves by picking lice off themselves and dropping them through the grating upon us and the crew below. Crawford had some money and he got two or three bottles of porter and gave me some, and I thought I never tasted anything so delicious before.

I found a man on board who had been a time keeper on a large job on a railway in France when I worked in the same place. He was bedroom steward on the Colombo, and we had great yarns about old times.

The steamship *Colombo* was used extensively during the war, towing two Artillery barges during the landing.

We started off again very early the next morning, and reached the fleet that day as they lay off Kimburn. We had a good view of the captured fort and could see the smoke made by our troops and the French burning some villages and corn up the river. The master's mate, boatswain and Men-of-War's men were removed to the flagship this day, and the next day, about 12 o'clock, an order came for us to be sent on board the Agamemnon. When we got on board all the sergeants were sent to the sergeants' mess and the remainder of the men were distributed among the different messes of the ship's company. We left all the sailors who had been with us and the Maltese on board the Colombo, and they were sent to Constantinople.

We sailed the same evening and arrived at Kamiesh on the 25th. We found the Agamemnon a fine vessel and a good lot of men for her ship's company. I admired their manner of pulling ropes to the tune of a fiddle. The fiddler was exempted from all other duties but fiddling, and would scrape away with great energy. The pea soup and plum duff went down very nicely after so long an absence, and the crew took care we should have plenty of it. They treated us with great kindness during our short voyage.

Flagship of the Black Sea fleet, H.M.S. *Agamemnon*, was the first screw ship of the line to be designed as such. She carried 90 guns, was 252 feet long, 36 feet wide and had a complement of 820.

In 1857 she assisted in laying the Atlantic cable and in 1870 was sold for £10,181, having been launched in 1842.

On the 26th Capt. Torrens of my own regiment came for us. He was an aide-de-camp to General Codrington and had been sent to march us up to Headquarters. We were landed in two boats for now the sailors and Maltese had left us there was not above 60 of us soldiers. We had a bad march up to Headquarters, for our new wellington boots drew our feet greatly and many of the men were crippled through them.

Capt. H. d'O Torrens had been slightly wounded and was mentioned in despatches, at Inkerman, where he was attached as acting Brigade Major to his father, Major General Sir Arthur Torrens.

He later became Major General, C.B., commanding the Belfast District.

We reached headquarters at about 6 o'clock that night and here the cavalry left us to proceed to Balaclava, and I and Crawford had a bottle of Porter each at parting, Crawford paying the shot for it. We halted here about half an hour and then was put under the care of another officer to be left at our different regiments.

The place was much altered since I left and had I been left to myself I should never have found my way to the Light Division, but we reached our regiment about half past eight—the bugles had just finished sounding the Last Post—and were given over to our adjutant. The news soon spread through the regiment of our return and they cheered us. I was soon surrounded by old comrades and dragged off to the canteen.

The 23rd remained in the Crimea until 14th June 1856 when, with the 33rd regiment, they embarked on H.M.S. *London* (ninety guns) arriving at Spithead on the 17th July. On the 21st they disembarked at Gosport and marched to Aldershot; and, on the 31st, the regiment was inspected by the Queen. On 1st February 1857 orders were received to proceed to China.

3252 Sergeant George Newman was not, however, with them. On the 1st January 1857 he went on furlough and no further record of him exists.

mborn, we had a good view of the [captur]
[...] Smoke made by our Troops and the Frenc[h]
[...]s and Corn up the river; Tw Masters Mate
[...] Wars then were removed to the Flag Ship th[...]
[ab]out 12 o Clock an order Came for us to be Sen[t]
[...]noon; When we got on board the Agame[mnon]
[...]re Sent to the Sergeants Mess and the remai[n]
[...]distributed among the different Messes of the
[...] the Sailors who had been with us and the
the Colombo, and they Were Sent to Constan[t]
the Same Evening and arrived at Kam[...]
found the Agamemnon a fine Vessel and [...]
Ships Company, I admired their Manner [...]
[...] tune of a fiddle, The Fiddler Was exemp[t]
[...]d but fiddling, and Would Scrape away w[...]
[...]up and Plum duff went down very Nice[...]
[...] and the Crew took Care we Should have [...]
[...]e us with great kindness during our Short [...]
[...] about Mid-day Captain Torrens of My ow[n]
[...] he Was an Aid-de-Camp to General Codri[ngton]
[...] Sent to March us up to the head Quarter[s]
[...] two boats, for Now the Sailors and Mat[...]
[...]as not above 60 of us Soldiers, we had a [...]
[...]e Quarters for our New Wellington Boots [...]
[...]e Many of the Men Were crippled throug[h]

BIBLIOGRAPHY

There are many easily accessible books on the Crimean War and Southern Russia. In addition to these I have consulted a number which are not so readily available. Among them are:

The Crimean War

"From the Fleet in the Fifties", by a Midshipman aboard H.M.S. *Queen*, 1902.

"The war in the Crimea", by General Sir Edward Hanby, 1894.

"The English Prisoners in Russia", by the 1st Lt. of H.M.S. *Tiger*.

"One of the Six Hundred", by Private J. W. Wightman, published in "The Nineteenth Century", 1892.

"The Crimean War from First to Last", by General Sir Daniel Lysons, 1895.

"Kars and our Captivity in Russia", by Sir Harry Atwell Lake, 1856.

"Reminiscences of Crimean Campaigning and Russian Imprisonment", by R. S. Farquharson, 1883.

Southern Russia

"Travels in the Eastern Caucasus, on the Caspian and Black Sea, During the Summer of 1871", by Lt. Gen. Sir Arthur Cunnynghame, 1872.

"Russian Shores of the Black Sea in the Autumn of 1852", by Laurence Oliphant, 1853.

"The Crimea and Odessa; Journal of a Tour", by Charles Koch, 1855.

"Russia on the Black Sea and the Sea of Azov", by H. D. Seymour, M.P., 1855.

"Travels in Southern Russia", by Xavier Hommaire de Hell, 1847.

INDEX

* These Regiments bore different titles in 1854. For the benefit of the general reader their more familiar titles have been used here and in the text.